BMW Z cars
Roadsters and Coupes

A design and development history

Other books by the author

BMW Z cars
Roadsters and Coupes

A design and development history

by Jackie Jouret

ID Media LLC
Portland, Oregon, USA

First published in the United States of America in 2021
by ID Media LLC

Printed in the United States of America

ISBN: 978-1-7333878-7-3

Typeset in Avenir

ID Media LLC
PO Box 96321
Portland, OR 97296 USA

Table of Contents

Z cars
The fun BMWs

Roadster…

The name alone tells you it's going to be fun, conveying a jaunty, lighthearted rhythm that suits these sporty two-seaters perfectly.

Like most automotive terms, "roadster" derives from the age of horse-drawn transportation. In this case, it refers to the horse itself, here one deemed suitable for travel. The term made its way to wheeled transportation via the bicycle, but it soon found a new purpose in describing a particularly exciting form of automobile. As reported by *The New York Times* on August 20, 1916, the Nomenclature Division of the US-based Society of Automotive Engineers defined a roadster as "an open car seating two or three. It may have additional seats on running boards or in rear deck."

Roadsters became synonymous with racing, whether by gentlemen drivers competing on the public-road circuits of Europe or professionals racing on US ovals like Indianapolis.

By the time BMW became a carmaker by buying the Eisenach Motor Works in October 1928, the company already had a strong sporting tradition on two wheels. Having started as a builder of aero engines during World War I, BMW moved into the motorcycle sector in 1923. The company began racing its motorcycles as soon as it began building them, and by 1925 it was offering race-ready sport bikes to customers.

Upon purchasing Eisenach, one of BMW's first moves was to introduce a roadster variant of its new 3/15. The wasp-tailed Wartburg set the stage for a series of roadsters (and coupes) that followed, and which put BMW at the forefront of European sports car racing in the 1930s.

Those developments came to an end with World War II, but a roadster would be central to BMW's postwar resurrection. In 1956, BMW offered the 507, a high-end Grand Touring roadster that became legendary as one of the most beautiful cars ever built, and certainly the most beautiful BMW. In 1959, however, the 507 was retired, having sold just a fraction of its expected volume.

BMW continued to offer convertible versions of its mainstream cars, but by the mid-1960s these were falling afoul of safety regulations, particularly in the US. Roll bar-equipped "targas" kept convertibles alive, but even the roadster-loving British carmakers had

abandoned the body style by 1980.

As the decade progressed, though, roadsters experienced an unexpected revival. BMW's Z1 concept made a big splash at the Frankfurt show in 1987, and Mazda's MX-5 Miata created a sensation at Chicago two years later. While the expensively hand-built Z1 remained a low-volume proposition, the affordable Miata had widespread appeal. More than 400,000 examples had been sold by the time the first-generation Miata finished its run in 1997, and countless manufacturers had responded with mainstream roadsters of their own.

Naturally, BMW was among them, and the success of its own Z3 meant that roadsters have had a permanent place in the lineup ever since. The Z-cars have become larger, heavier, and more sophisticated over the years, but they continue to represent the essence of BMW, and to exist for the sheer fun of driving.

This is the story of those cars, and a few more that embody the same exuberant spirit even if they don't have a Z as part of their model names.

To tell it, I've been helped immeasurably by a number of current and former BMW executives and employees, all of whom took time out of their busy schedules to answer my questions, double-check information, and supply me with images.

This book would not have been possible without input from two people, in particular: David Carp and Chris Bangle.

Carp joined BMW in 1992, after graduating from Art Center College of Design, and he's made important contributions to cars including the Z8, E63/E64 6 Series, and several Rolls-Royce automobiles. Since 2019, Carp has been team leader for BMW's Design Identity and Media department, a role that dovetails perfectly with Carp's passion for design history. For the past 20+ years, Carp has been saving invaluable documents that now form the BMW Design Archive. The Archive is an essential research tool for understanding how BMW's cars came to be, one that's complemented by Carp's evidence-based approach to historical research.

For this book, Carp dug up rare images, read nearly every chapter in this book, corrected mistakes and filled in gaps in my knowledge with tact and good humor.

Chris Bangle (another Art Center alumnus) served as BMW's design chief from 1992 through 2009, steering the company in a distinctly modern direction that didn't always sit well with BMW's traditional audience. Even so, Bangle helped the company grow in size and sophistication, and much of what BMW Design accomplished under Bangle's leadership has since become industry standard. He deserves credit for moving the game forward in ways that most of us will never perceive, much less appreciate.

For this book, Bangle was extraordinarily generous with his assistance, taking time out from his work at Chris Bangle & Associates to answer countless questions, read chapters, make corrections, and illuminate my understanding of events that affected the outcome of BMW's automobiles.

I'd also like to thank Dr. Ulrich Bez, Dr. Burkhard Göschel, Joji Nagashima, Anders Warming, and Erik Wensberg for taking the time to talk to me in the spring of 2021.

Where other subjects of this book are concerned, I was able to rely on interviews conducted during my editorship of *Bimmer* magazine from 1999 to 2016, many of which had remained unpublished until now. Thanks to Klaus Draeger, Klaus Fröhlich, Heinz Krusche, Juliane Blasi, Nadya Arnaout, and Adrian van Hooydonk for their conversation at press launches for the Z8, E85 Z4 and M Roadster, E89 Z4, i8 Roadster, and many other BMW automobiles.

Finally, I'd like to thank Helmut Werb for images, along with Marc Thiesbürger and Ruth Standfuss at the BMW Archive. The latter constitutes a remarkable source of rare images and other documentation, and an invaluable resource for those of us researching BMW history.

—*Jackie Jouret*

Pre-Z: BMW roadsters of the 1930s and '50s

Established in 1916, BMW was already a highly regarded manufacturer of airplane engines and race-winning motorcycles when it added automobiles to its portfolio on November 14, 1928. Following a few ill-fated attempts to build a car from scratch, BMW purchased Germany's third-oldest car maker, the Eisenach *Fahrzeugfabrik* (Vehicle Factory) some 250 miles north of Munich.

At the time, Eisenach was building the British-designed Austin Seven under license and selling it under its own Dixi nameplate as the 3/15 DA1. To unpack that nomenclature, 3/15 referenced the car's 3-horsepower tax classification and 15-horsepower engine output, and DA1 stood for *Deutsche Ausführung*, or German Version 1.

Although the Dixi was popular, it fell short of BMW's exacting technical standards. Almost immediately upon taking over the factory, BMW's engineers began updating the car with modern features. Though it retained the 748cc Austin engine, the first BMW-badged automobile had a more spacious all-steel body in place of aluminum-over-wood construction, plus four-wheel brakes and hand-crank windows.

On August 7, 1929—a mere four weeks after the first BMW car rolled off the production line—BMW entered a trio of its 3/15 PS (for *Pferdstarke*, a German measurement of horsepower) DA2 models in one of Europe's most grueling reliability tests. The *International Alpenfahrt*, or International Alpine Rally, ran from Munich to Milan via a 1,646-mile route that included nineteen Alpine passes.

The cars entered by BMW were no ordinary 3/15 sedans but prototypes of a forthcoming two-seater with a folding top and a truncated tail. These brand-new BMWs finished the rally on time and in fine style, setting the fastest times over both special stages to win the Golden Alpine Trophy. The trio returned to Eisenach crowned in laurels (**opposite**), having made a dramatic statement of BMW's arrival as a carmaker.

3/15 DA3 Wartburg: BMW's first roadster

By the spring of 1930, BMW's new "Wartburg" roadster was ready for public consumption. Named for the castle that looms above Eisenach, the Wartburg had no rear seat or luggage compartment, just a wasp-like tail that gave it a decidedly racy appearance.

It also had a new version of the 748cc engine. This DA3 version had a 7.0:1 compression ratio instead of 5.6:1, a larger Solex carburetor, and twenty percent more power: 18 horsepower at 3,500 rpm and 26 pound-feet at 3,000 rpm where the DA2 put out just 15 horsepower at 3,000 rpm and 25 pound-feet at 2,000 rpm. As those numbers indicate, the DA3 liked to rev, producing peak horsepower and torque at higher rpm than the DA2.

Just as important to performance, the two-seat Wartburg weighed just 902 pounds—165 fewer than the 1,067-pound 3/15 sedan. All of that added up to a top speed of 60 mph, quite fast for any small car in 1930.

On April 13, 1930, a trio of Wartburgs entered the Brandenburg endurance trial, driven by a team from the Berlin police department's sports club. Led by Captain Erwin Sander, the police team finished the rally on time and with no penalties, scoring an important victory for BMW's new roadster.

One month later, the Wartburg was offered to the public for RM 3,100 ($740), more expensive than a standard 3/15 cabriolet but still attainable by Germans of ordinary means. The Wartburg was declared "a fabulous small German sports car" by *Motor and Sport* magazine, and it proved its mettle by winning a number of hillclimbs that summer.

One Wartburg was purchased by Hermann Kohlrausch, a master dyer in Eisenach. Kohlrausch bought the Wartburg for his 26-year-old son, Robert, as an inducement to race on four wheels rather than two. "Bobby" Kohlrausch had spent 1923 as an apprentice at the Eisenach plant, inspiring him to study engineering while racing motorcycles.

The younger Kohlrausch modified his new car's engine by machining the cylinder head for higher compression. He also fabricated his own exhaust system and fitted a larger Solex carb.

Entering his first race with the modified Wartburg at Kesselberg on June 15, 1930, Kohlrausch won, setting a new class record in the process. He followed by winning the Würgau, Gaisberg, and Oberjoch hillclimbs, then finished second at the Nürburgring that summer to cement his status as one of Germany's premier racers in the under-750cc class.

For 1931, BMW provided Kohlrausch with a factory-prepared Wartburg with a prototype overhead-valve engine. He won twelve of the fifteen races he entered with that car, including the Neroberg race in which he's shown here (**opposite, below**). Kohlrausch was BMW's first "star" racer on four wheels, and his victories helped the young marque make a big impression on sports-minded car buyers.

BMW sold 150 examples of its diminutive sports car before production ended in 1931. Despite that modest volume, the Wartburg played an outsized role in BMW's reputation as a maker of quick, agile-handling automobiles.

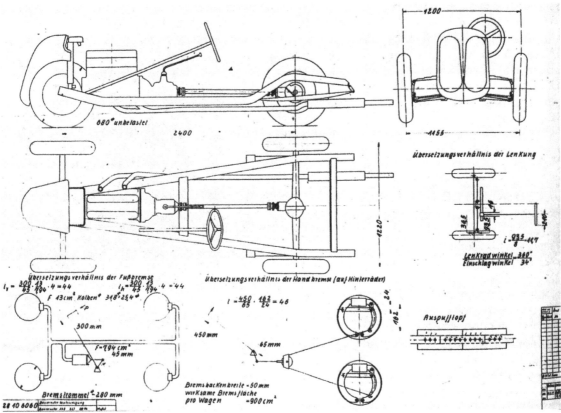

303: Building for the future

Despite its success with the Wartburg, BMW didn't build another roadster immediately. Instead, the company concentrated its engineering resources on its first all-new car, the 303 (left) that would revolutionize the auto industry while providing BMW with an enduring template for its own automobiles.

The prevailing wisdom held that a heavier car would have better roadholding than a lighter one, but Fritz Fiedler believed otherwise. Fiedler designed the 303's chassis under the principle of *Leichtbau*, or "lightweight construction," which endowed the 303 and all of the BMWs that followed with exceptional handling.

As shown in the engineering drawings at left, he designed the 303 with a stiff-but-light tubular A-shaped frame, rack-and-pinion steering, and compliant suspension. At the front, single wishbones were controlled by a transverse leaf spring with hydraulic dampers; at the rear, a live axle on longitudinal leaf springs was paired with lever-type dampers. Along with those elements, the chassis had low unsprung weight, which let the suspension work more freely. It also had strong brakes to match the 1,182cc M78a six-cylinder engine designed by Rudolf Schleicher and Karl Rech. With 5.6:1 compression and a pair of Solex 26 FV carburetors, the M78a (right) put out 30 horsepower at 4,000 rpm and 51 pound-feet at 2,000 rpm.

The 303 featured a long hood to accommodate the engine, and a cabin placed farther to the rear. The fenders arched gracefully over the wheels, and the front featured a chrome-trimmed grille whose shape gave it the nickname "double kidneys." (Coachbuilder Ihle offered a double-kidney retrofit for the 3/15, leading later observers to conclude incorrectly that Ihle, not BMW, had created the design.) Instead of a hood ornament, the car's nose was capped by a flush-mounted BMW roundel.

Introduced at the 1933 Berlin auto show, the 303 announced BMW's true arrival as a carmaker. A few weeks later, a team of 303s performed flawlessly in the 2,000 Kilometers of Germany rally, just as their 3/15 predecessors

had in the *International Alpenfahrt* four years earlier. Like those cars, the 303s displayed exemplary handling, balanced performance, and exceptional reliability, virtues that became indelibly associated with BMW in the prewar era.

With its *Alpenfahrt* victory, the 303 made a strong statement of BMW's sporting ambitions, but it wasn't an end in itself. Indeed, the car would provide the basis for an entire line of new BMWs in a variety of body styles, and with ever-more-powerful 1.5- and 1.9-liter six-cylinder engines.

At the very next Berlin auto show in March 1934, BMW surprised everyone with a pair of roadster prototypes set among BMW's sedans and cabriolets. The company hadn't yet decided whether to build either of these prototypes, but the favorable reaction of show goers and BMW dealers provided a convincing argument.

Das Eifelrennen auf dem Nürburgring am 16. Juni 1935 und das X. Internat. Kesselbergrennen am 30. Juni 1935

2 große Triumphe für BMW

v. Delius erringt im Eifelrennen auf BMW 6 Zyl.-Sportwagen den

1. Preis

der Sportwagenklasse bis 2000 ccm und fährt die

beste Zeit aller Sportwagenklassen

In der Klasse bis 1500 ccm erringen 3 BMW-Sport den

2. 3. und 4. Preis

Im X. intern. Kesselbergrennen erringt v. Delius auf BMW 6 Zylinder-Sportwagen den

1. Preis

in der Klasse der Sportwagen 1500 bis 2000 ccm.

Die fast ununterbrochene Reihe glanzvoller Siege beweist aufs neue die Güte des Materials, die vorbildliche Konstruktion und Leistungsfähigkeit des BMW 6 Zyl.-Sportwagens. Ihm gehört die Zukunft.

Bild oben:
v. Delius nach seinem großen Sieg im Blumenkranz.
Bild rechts:
v. Delius in einer Kurve der Kesselberg-Rennstrecke.

BAYERISCHE MOTOREN WERKE AG MÜNCHEN 13

315/1 & 319/1: The first sporting sixes

Dubbed the 315/1 and 319/1, the low-slung, swoopy roadsters looked fast even on the Berlin show stand, which was precisely the point where Rudolf Schleicher was concerned.

Having engineered BMW's race-winning motorcycles in the 1920s, Schleicher spent a few years at automaker Horch before returning to BMW. After leading the motorcycle division back to racing glory, Schleicher aimed to do the same for its automobiles. He'd already enlarged the M78a engine to 1,490cc in the standard 315 that debuted in Berlin alongside the new roadsters, but its 34 horsepower weren't enough for a real sports racer. For the M315/1, Schleicher replaced its single Solex 26 BFLV with a trio of Solex 26 BFRH carburetors, increased compression from 5.6:1 to 6.8:1, and gave it more radical valve timing. That increased output to 40 horsepower—enough to make the 315/1 a genuine contender in the 1.5-liter sports car class.

Fiedler's tube-frame chassis was certainly up to the task, especially with the ride height lowered and the suspension stiffened. The bodywork looked like a winner, too, designed (most likely) and constructed by Reutter of Stuttgart with a neat, aerodynamic sports car shape.

The roadsters drew rave reviews in Berlin, and BMW was buoyed sufficiently by the response to put the 315/1 into production. On July 21, 1934 a trio of factory-entered 315/1 roadsters finished the 2,000 Kilometers of Germany having won a gold medal apiece. Two weeks later, the three roadsters were equally dominant in the *International Alpenfahrt*. BMW won the team trophy, while Ernst von Delius won the overall competition for individual drivers.

Despite its high price—RM 5,200, or $2,047—the roadster attracted 242 enthusiastic customers from 1934 to 1936. Many 315/1s were raced, and the car proved highly competitive in the 1.5-liter junior category.

In 1935, BMW followed with the 319/1, with a 1,911cc that vaulted it into the premier 2.0-liter class for sports cars. In the 1930s as today, sports car racing was the province mainly of enthusiasts, with a smattering of paid professional drivers against whom talented amateurs could measure their performance.

One was von Delius, who'd joined BMW's factory team to race the 315/1. Moving up to the 319/1 for 1935, von Delius took advantage of the car's higher top speed—81 mph—to win at the Nürburgring *Eifelrennen* as well as the Kesselberg hillclimb.

BMW celebrated his feats with a "win ad" (**opposite, lower left**) which noted that von Delius had posted the fastest lap time of all sports cars at the 'Ring that year. "The almost uninterrupted series of brilliant victories again proves the quality of the material, the exemplary construction and efficiency of the BMW. He owns the future."

Since all nouns and pronouns have a gender in German, it's hard to know whether the "he" refers to the car or von Delius. In any case, the future looked bright for both driver and BMW. Von Delius would graduate to a Grand Prix drive with Auto Union, and he scored a series of strong results in 1936 and 1937 before an unfortunate accident at the Nürburgring put him in the hospital with what appeared to be minor injuries. That assessment was incorrect, and he died a day later at age 25.

While at BMW, von Delius had done more than just win key races. His success with the 315/1 helped forge a relationship between BMW and HJ Aldington, resulting in BMW's first exports to Britain. Having been beaten by the BMWs himself, Aldington negotiated the licensed production of right-hand drive BMWs in England, where they'd be sold as Frazer Nash-BMWs...a mere two years after BMW had ceased building Austin Sevens under license.

The 315/1 and 319/1 would remain popular throughout their production run, and the 315/1 was still competitive a few years later, when young BMW engineer Alex von Falkenhausen got one of his own. Seen in the photo opposite, lower right, von Falkenhausen would become one of BMW's longest-tenured and best-loved engineers.

For von Falkenhausen and BMW, the 315/1 and 319/1 were but a prelude. The real excitement still lay ahead.

328: The real-deal racer

On Saturday, June 13, 1936, BMW's factory race team arrived at the Nürburgring, where a 2.0-liter sports car race was being held in support of the German Grand Prix. Along with its 319/1s, the team brought the prototype of an all-new roadster, one that had never been seen outside the factory gates at Eisenach.

Identified as the 328, the car was clearly much racier than the 319/1. Its bodywork—credited to Fritz Fiedler and Peter Szymanowski, but clearly an evolution of the earlier car's Reutter coachwork—was more sleekly aerodynamic. Its headlights were integrated with the front fenders for reduced drag, and the fenders themselves flowed more cleanly into the body. It also had drilled aluminum knock-off wheels for low unsprung weight and faster tire changes.

Created on a very tight budget, the 328 relied on what historian Rainer Simons called "known features in new relationships." While that was most obvious in its 303-based chassis—with the same 94.5-inch wheelbase as the 315/1 and 319/1—it was also apparent under the hood. Conceived by Rudolf Schleicher, the M328 combined the 1,971cc block sourced from BMW's upscale 326 sedan with a new cylinder head designed by Rudolf Flemming with hemispherical combustion chambers and an ingenious valve train arrangement. With a compression ratio of 7.5:1 and a trio of Solex carburetors, the M328 delivered 80 horsepower at 4,500 rpm and 96 pound-feet at 3,500 rpm. Top speed for this 1,830-pound roadster was a very fast 93 mph.

At the 'Ring, the new roadster was driven by Ernst Henne (**opposite**), BMW's speed-record superhero on two wheels. In front of some 250,000 spectators, Henne averaged 63.1 mph over five laps and nearly 70 miles of racing, beating the second-place (and supercharged) Alfa Romeo 6C 1750 by nearly 2.5 *minutes*.

Henne and the new 328 became the talk of the paddock, overshadowing even the Mercedes-Auto Union Grand Prix duel that took place later that day. It was the beginning of an unprecedented run that would yield hundreds of 2.0-liter sports car victories—including a considerable number for HJ Aldington and his star driver AFP Fane in Britain, helping BMW cement its status in that vital export market.

Equally significant was the 328's development into a pair of aerodynamic coupes, one with bodywork developed in-house at BMW and the other by Touring of Milan (**below**). Both displayed exceptional aerodynamics, and the Touring-bodied coupe scored a class win/fifth overall at Le Mans in 1938 before winning the *Gran Premio di Brescia* (aka Mille Miglia) outright in 1940.

Shortly after the BMW factory team staged a victory parade in downtown Munich, World War II brought racing to a halt, along with nearly all civilian automobile production.

By then, BMW had built 464 examples of its 328, which Schleicher and Fiedler had regarded only as a stopgap model. They'd begun working on its successor almost immediately, and their new sports car was set to feature lower, wider bodywork, an updated chassis, and a powerful new engine designed in large part by Alex von Falkenhausen.

World events would intervene before that car was completed, but not before the 328 roadster had cemented BMW's status as a maker of lithe, agile, and well-balanced sports cars that performed as well in racing as they did on the road. Once racing resumed, the 328 remained competitive in the 2.0-liter sports car class throughout the 1950s, a testament to the quantum leap BMW had made with its creation.

528 & 507: Postwar Grand Touring

Thanks to its role as a supplier of aircraft engines to the German military, BMW became a target of Allied bombing raids in the final years of World War II. By 1945, the company was in ruins. BMW managed to survive, but the company didn't begin building cars again until 1951. When it did, the company started with a large sedan rather than a roadster, as its executives decreed a sports car inappropriate for still war-ravaged Germany. By March 1954, however, a roadster was back on the agenda, though this time BMW would build a stylish and substantial Grand Touring car rather than a lightweight racer.

Initially designated the 528, the new roadster (**opposite, top**) shared its basic chassis and V8 engine with the 501 sedan. Its bodywork was derived in part from the Mille Miglia Roadster designed by BMW design chief Wilhelm Meyerhuber in 1940, and it also carried strong echoes of the 328-based racers built by Ernst Loof's independent Veritas firm after 1945. That wasn't surprising, given that Loof had returned to the BMW fold after Veritas' demise; from his shop at the Nürburgring, Loof was responsible for developing the new roadster.

The 528 began testing at the Nürburgring in August 1954. Shortly thereafter, New York importer Max Hoffman met with BMW executives at Baur in Stuttgart to discuss importing BMW's V8 powered sedans and the forthcoming sports car. There, he saw the 528 in the metal or in photos and proclaimed it so ugly as to be unsaleable, particularly in the US. To rectify the situation, Hoffman put BMW in touch with a young German-born American designer named Albrecht von Goertz. Within a few months, the car had been redesigned as the 507 (**opposite, below**).

From its debut at Frankfurt in September 1955, the 507 has been widely considered one of the most beautiful cars ever created, and certainly the most beautiful BMW. Its performance was somewhat less stellar than its looks, however: Despite having 150 horsepower and 177 pound-feet from its 3,168cc V8 engine, the 507 was more *boulevardier* than thoroughbred. Hans Stuck Sr. managed a few hillclimb victories in a pair of 507s prepared by Alex von Falkenhausen, but the car wasn't all that sporty. Despite a top speed of 137 mph, it wasn't suited to circuit racing like the 328 had been.

Nonetheless, its glamorous appearance and high-revving V8 engine made the 507 one of the most prestigious road cars of its era. Motorcycle Grand Prix champion John Surtees got one, while others were purchased by Elvis Presley (who gave another 507 to Ursula Andress as a gift), David Carradine, King Constantine II of Greece, Prince Rainier of Monaco, and the Aga Khan.

Despite its celebrity appeal, the 507 was doomed by production problems and faulty sales projections, not to mention an astronomical sales price: nearly $10,000 in the US. From 1956 through 1959, BMW built just 254 examples of its first postwar roadster, including the 528 prototype.

Like the 328, the 507 was an epoch-defining roadster for BMW. It was also the last of the breed: Once the final 507 left the Munich assembly plant, BMW wouldn't build another roadster for nearly three decades.

Z1
Freedom on four wheels

Before we discuss BMW's re-entry into the roadster segment, let's address a widespread rumor about the Z1. Despite what several authors—including myself prior to being corrected on the matter by Dr. Karlheinz Lange—the "Z" in Z1 does not stand for *Zukunft*, the German word for "future."

We'll get to what it *does* mean shortly; first, let's consider what was going on within BMW, and across the automotive industry as a whole, as the Z1 was being conceived.

As mentioned in the previous chapter, BMW had abandoned the roadster segment in 1959, when the 507 was discontinued after three short years in production. The expense of the 507's development, along with other revenue-sapping activities, had driven BMW to near-bankruptcy by late 1959. The company was nearly sold to Mercedes that December, but a life-saving investment by Herbert Quandt allowed BMW to retain its independence. The company rebuilt its product line around the 700 microcar followed by the *Neue Klasse* 1500 sedan and the Type 114 two-door sold as the 1600-2 and 2002. The Type 114 was also offered as a Baur-built convertible, first as the fully open *Vollcabriolet* and then with a targa-style roll bar for additional safety.

All of those cars were highly successful, and the profits they generated allowed BMW to expand and modernize throughout the 1960s and '70s. In the latter decade, BMW rationalized its product lineup with the now-familiar 3, 5, 6, and 7 Series automobiles; like the Type 114, the first-generation 3 Series was available as a Baur TC1 cabriolet alongside the factory-built two-door hardtop.

As BMW's only top-down driving option, the TC1 was a niche product, and only 4,595 were built from 1977 to 1981. Nonetheless, Baur carried on with its TC2 when the E21 was superseded by the E30 3 Series in 1982. This proved far more popular, and in 1986 BMW demonstrated its commitment to open-air motoring by taking convertible production in-house. Whether built by Baur or BMW, however, these four-seat convertibles retained the essential character of their hardtop counterparts. Save for the wind in one's hair, they were no more energetic or fun to drive.

Convertibles were nice, but the roadster remained the purest expression of driving fun, at least until safety concerns—and the decline of the British auto industry—caused roadsters to all but disappear by the early 1980s. Of the final holdouts, the Lotus Elan was discontinued in 1975, followed by the Triumph Spitfire and TR7 in 1980. Fiat X1/9 production ended in 1982, though the model would cling grimly to life at coachbuilder Bertone before giving up the ghost in 1989.

Even so, enthusiasts continued to desire a lightweight two-seat sports car. In 1982, a small team at Mazda's Southern California outpost began developing a lightweight sports car. Led by Bob Hall and Mark Jordan, Mazda's engineers and designers wanted to recapture the spirit of the old British two-seaters, but with modern styling and safety matched to Japanese reliability and quality control. The car they created would become known as the Mazda MX-5, aka the Miata.

BMW Technik GmbH: BMW's think tank

While Hall and Jordan had put their team together for the express purpose of building a roadster, Dr. Ulrich Bez (**below**) had gathered a group of BMW personnel together in Munich for a different mission altogether: creating the company's first in-house think tank.

Born in Bad Canstatt in 1943, Bez earned his undergraduate engineering degree from the University of Stuttgart, followed by a doctorate from the Free University of Berlin. After joining Porsche in 1972, he eventually became that carmaker's director of vehicle research.

In 1982, Bez was recruited to BMW by Dr. Karlheinz Radermacher, board member for research and development, and chairman Eberhard von Kuenheim. In Munich, he'd head a new department for advanced development. Two years later, on a Thursday evening, Bez

Photo courtesy BMW Archive

received a phone call from Dr. Hans Hagen, who'd replaced Radermacher as head of R&D when the latter left BMW for ZF in 1983. Hagen had an interesting proposal: Would Bez be interested in heading up a new subsidiary within BMW?

"I don't know who proposed me for the job, but it was von Kuenheim's idea to establish a 'spin-off' company working outside the more or less stubborn management culture," Bez told me in 2021. "Hagen said the spin-off would have no specific target, but a budget of DM 10 million per year…no further direction about where to be, what to do, or whom to work with, only that the work should be in the automotive field. He told me to think about it, and I assumed I'd have the coming weekend to consider. Instead, he called me at 8 a.m. the next morning asking if I'd decided. I had five seconds to answer: Yes."

Bez assembled a team and moved his new department into a rented industrial building on Hanauer Strasse, separated from the four-cylinder headquarters building by the greenery of Munich's Olympiapark. There, they began working on a variety of topics small and large, among them a V8 engine to replace the long-running M30 "big six." (That engine went into production as the M60 in 1992.)

In January 1985, the group was organized into a subsidiary, BMW Technik GmbH. As a *Gesellschaft mit beschränkter Haftung*, or limited-liability company, BMW Technik had a considerable degree of independence from BMW AG (*Aktiengesellschaft*, or publicly-held corporation), even as it was wholly owned by the parent corporation. Its mission was "to develop innovative, future-oriented and original overall vehicle concepts and sub-concepts away from the constraints of a specific series workflow schedule. However, the objective should always be to develop solutions that have the potential for series development."

Working outside the normal structure, BMW Technik could develop ideas from the ground up, rather than on assignment from the board of management. In that way, it could anticipate BMW's future needs for series production, and exploring the possibilities offered by new materials and technologies. Just as important, BMW Technik's unique structure allowed it to work much faster than normal, thanks to constant communication and cooperation between departments that were siloed away from one another in the parent company. Engineering and design would proceed together, while supply-chain management, cost accounting, and production would be involved at an earlier stage to ensure feasibility.

BMW Technik's first major project began in the spring of 1985 as an exploration of "freedom on four wheels." The project became known as "Z1" thanks to a numbering system devised by Dr. Bez, and which was derived from BMW Technik's internal designation as ZT. (The internal designations for all BMW subsidiaries begin with the letter Z; departments are organized under the board member to whom they report: A for the chairman, E for development or *Entwicklung*, and so on.)

"I decided to follow a strict project management strategy," Dr. Bez told me in 2021. "We would give big projects a single-digit number, medium projects a double-digit number, and smaller projects a three-digit number. To give it a BMW Technik character, we added a Z in front, so Z1, Z10, Z100, etc. Each project came with a target, milestones, and a budget. '*Freiheit auf vier Rädern*' ["freedom on four wheels"] became the first big project, and if you look at the design highlights, especially the side, you can see a lot of 'Z' highlights. When the project became reality, we could not find a better, more characteristic name, consequently it remained the Z1."

The name had nothing to do with the German word *Zukunft*, but the car itself had everything to do with the future.

Freedom, defined

Beyond the name, the project's outcome was determined by the concept behind it.

"We took the term 'freedom' literally," said BMW Technik design chief Harm Lagaaij—sometimes spelled Lagaay, though Lagaaij is the original spelling in his native Dutch. Lagaaij

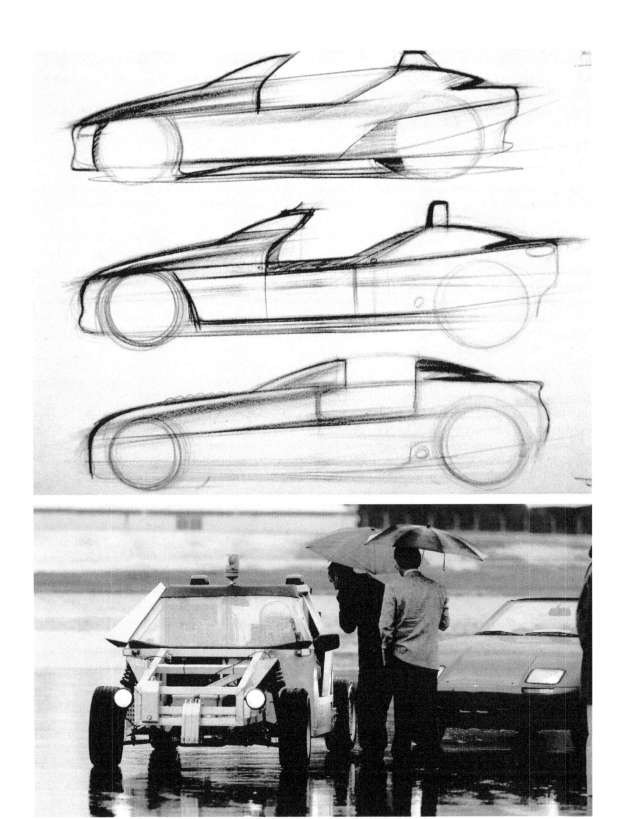

came to BMW Technik from Ford, where he'd been chief of design since 1977.

Speaking to former *Suddeutsche Zeitung* automotive editor Jürgen Lewandowski, Lagaaij elaborated. "At first, we didn't care where the engine was located, whether the occupants should have protection from a rain shower, or whether there was room for a trunk. When we started to use the term 'sheer driving pleasure,' we also thought of two-wheeled vehicles like four-wheeled vehicles. Why don't we try to achieve something in between? Feasibility wasn't a question at this point, just the working title of freedom on four wheels."

Early sketches proposed a four-wheeled motorcycle, an off-road adventure vehicle that required its occupants to wear helmets, and a rudimentary roadster. "Eventually," Lewandowski wrote in *Z1: The Roadster of the Future*, his 1989 model history, the team came up with "a 'sensible two seater,' comfortable but with the joy of driving, minimalist but suitable for everyday use, sensible and practical, rust-free, and also with cornering speeds to set all the alarm bells ringing at the competition."

The initial sketches for that car (**opposite, top**) were made by Ichiro Hatayama, a Japanese-born designer who arrived at BMW Technik in May 1985. Like Lagaaij, Hatayama came to Munich from Ford in Cologne; in 1986, he returned to Japan to work as an independent design consultant.

As everyone at Technik knew, the real fun of driving lay not at high speeds on the *autobahn* but in the corners, where a roadster excelled. One of the crucial concerns in achieving high cornering capabilities is engine placement. As Lagaaij noted, the Technik team didn't commit to a given drivetrain configuration at the outset, despite BMW's long history of front-engine, rear-wheel drive roadsters. Instead, they determined that a mid-engine design was better suited to achieving high cornering speeds and agile handling, thanks to the low polar moment of inertia that results from placing a vehicle's mass close to its center.

Once a mid-engine configuration was chosen, the question became whether to situate the engine fore or aft of the passenger compartment. A rear-mid configuration was the supercar standard, employed by cars like the Ferrari Testarossa, Maserati Miura, and BMW's own M1, but it tended to create a noisy, hot cockpit, and it complicated handling on snow and ice. And from a design standpoint, it didn't fit with the classic roadster form, which emphasized a long hood, short rear deck, and a passenger compartment set just ahead of the rear axle.

Although a front-mid engine configuration solved both passenger comfort and design issues, BMW Technik needed to test both engine placements before committing the Z1 to one or another. "We couldn't afford to build two prototypes," Bez told Lewandowski. "We had to build an experimental vehicle that demonstrated both driving states so that we could make the decision of what we wanted to build."

Mixing the new and the familiar

The experimental vehicle known as Z1E (**opposite, below**) was designed in three modules. The front contained the front axle and steering mechanism. The middle held the engine and gearbox, allowing these parts to be moved fore and aft. The final module held the rear axle, conferring a wheelbase that measured 2,415mm, or 95.1 inches.

For the axles themselves, BMW Technik started by digging into the 3 Series parts bin. The E30's MacPherson strut suspension worked well up front, though the BMW Technik chassis engineers led by Rudolf Müller adjusted track width and caster to work with wider wheels and 205/55-15 tires borrowed from the E30 M3.

The E30's semi-trailing arm rear suspension didn't fit well into the Z1 chassis, so Müller's team created the Z-axle, named not for the car but for its resemblance to the letter Z when viewed from a certain angle. A central-guided double wishbone system in aluminum, the Z-axle achieved the high lateral acceleration that was part of the Z1's mission from the beginning. At a claimed 1.0 g, grip was so high that it rivaled that of a Formula One car from just a few years earlier.

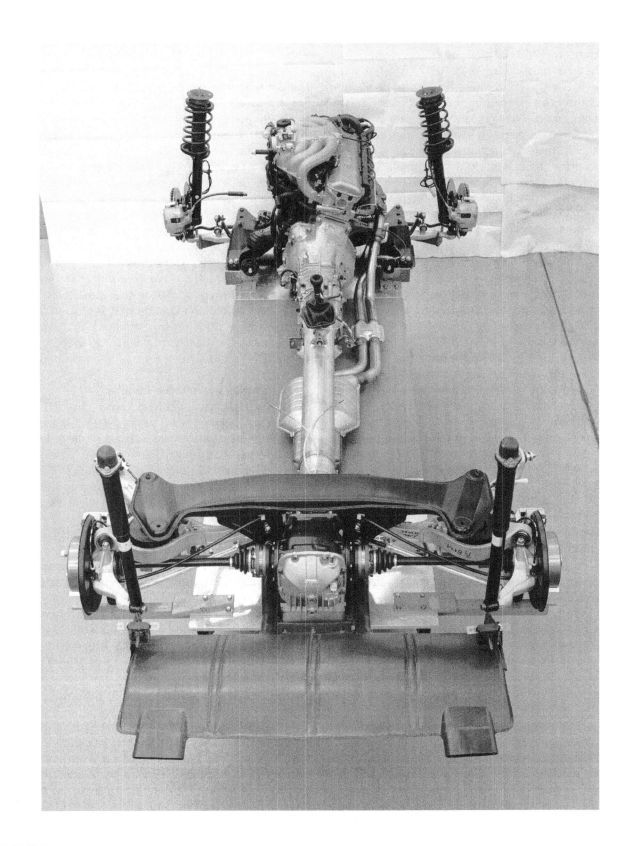

The powertrain was chosen early in the process. Technik decided to use the 2,494cc M20 "small six," paired with the familiar Getrag 260 five-speed manual transmission. With two valves per cylinder, the M20 featured BMW's first belt- rather than chain-driven camshafts. At its 1977 introduction, the engine displaced 2.0 liters and delivered 122 horsepower and 120 pound-feet; by September 1985, it had been enlarged to 2.5 liters. Equipped with Bosch Motronic digital motor electronics and a three-way catalytic converter, the M20 delivered a lively 170 horsepower at 5,800 rpm and 167 pound-feet at 4,300 rpm.

Smooth-running and responsive, the 2.5-liter M20 six was ideal for a modern roadster application. Making it fit between the Z1's front axle and the firewall required exceptional precision: Moving it into the ideal position caused the oil pump to collide with the axle, so the engineers borrowed the oil pump and pan arrangement from the all-wheel drive 325iX, which located the pump beneath the engine.

Once the car was functional, testing was conducted by a number of drivers, principally Dr. Bez (an experienced racer) and Finnish rally/race legend Rauno Aaltonen. On July 2, 1985, the team voted on their preference in several categories. The front mid-engine car won in every respect except aerodynamics and image, favored by the majority with respect to design/styling, driving dynamics, suitability for production/price, time required for development and production, packaging, and safety.

The latter consideration was important even though the car wasn't slated for production. As part of its mission, Technik had to consider such practical factors rather than simply building a dream car, so Alexander Pregl was tasked with making sure the vehicle would meet all legal requirements for use on the road.

Modern design, avant garde construction

With the drivetrain configuration finalized, Lagaaij's design team could advance from the preliminary sketches. As Lagaaij told Lewandowski, he was excited by "the opportunity to revisit a classic topic and reinterpret it. Although a rear mid-engine would have been attractive, this alternative attracted me a lot more."

Putting the Z1's engine up front allowed a modernization of traditional roadster proportions, with "a long, smoldering, leaning bonnet [hood], and a short, concise rear, which for decades had defined great sports cars."

Lagaaij had more freedom than most car designers, and not only because BMW Technik's structure permitted it. The need to accommodate just two people was liberating in itself, as was the minimal consideration given to trunk space. The only real constraint came from the dimensions of the six-cylinder engine, which was fairly tall as well as long.

The final design was dominated by horizontal lines, one of which extends from the front of the car all the way to the rear bumper. Above that line, the car curves upward to the rear deck, which is itself horizontal.

The horizontal line is formed in part by the door sills, which constitute the most visibly innovative aspect of the Z1's design. Even before the rest of the car had been drawn in detail, BMW Technik decided to use the drop-down doors designed by Klaus Gersmann. (Gersmann would patent the design in 1989.) The unusual doors helped the Z1 stand out from the crowd, much as the gull-wing doors had done on Mercedes' 300 SL coupe of the 1950s. They weren't just for show, however: They also made the body more rigid, reducing twist and self-steering and eliminating the need for a targa-style roll bar. (The Z1 has a roll bar, but not behind the seats. Instead, it runs through the A-pillars and across the top of the windshield.) Retracting halfway into the sills, Gersmann's doors improved side-impact protection, too.

The use of those doors was assumed to preclude any real future for the Z1, but the board reacted more favorably than expected when Bez and his team presented their work on November 26, 1985. Rather than kill the project, the board authorized the creation of a fully-functional prototype within six months.

Such a tight deadline could only be met thanks to the simultaneous development

of nearly every element, something that BMW Technik's unique structure allowed it to accomplish. Engineering proceeded alongside design, and also in concert with the supply-chain management that allowed BMW Technik to take advantage of the latest innovations by automotive suppliers worldwide.

One goal was to ensure that the Z1 undercut the weight of a 3 Series convertible by 200 kilograms, or 440 pounds. Since the car would borrow its drivetrain and other components from the 3 Series, it needed a new kind of chassis to reach its target weight. BMW Technik chose a self-supporting monocoque frame, which would be constructed in steel, then hot-dip galvanized to prevent rust. The zinc plating increased steel's rigidity by about 25 percent, particularly around the welded seams and overlap points, improving the car's handling in the process.

The Baur coachworks in Stuttgart would build the steel monocoque (**opposite, top**), while Messerschmitt-Bölkow-Blohm Plastics worked with BMW Technik to develop and produce the composite floor that would be glued and screwed onto the frame. Weighing just 33 pounds, the floor consisted of two layers of fiberglass-reinforced epoxy resin sandwiching a layer of polyurethane foam. Itself extremely rigid, it increased the torsional stiffness of the monocoque by ten percent, and it was reinforced at crucial areas like suspension pickup points and seat attachments.

Like a mid-engine drivetrain configuration, the monocoque helped centralize the Z1's mass, and so did the use of lightweight plastic for its outer skin. Light weight was only the first advantage of plastic bodywork: Plastic doesn't rust, obviously, and it has the further benefit of recovering its original shape following deformation—at least to a point.

For the Z1's exterior, BMW Technik chose Xenoy, a thermoplastic material developed and produced by General Electric Plastics. The bumpers were constructed from an even more elastic thermoplastic material that allowed them to spring back to their original shape following collisions of up to 2.5 mph. The hood, trunk lid,

and the cover panel for the convertible top were made of composite materials created by Swiss specialist Seger + Hoffman AG, a supplier of carbon fiber parts to the Sauber race team.

As another bonus, none of the plastic parts required any special preparation prior to painting. That said, they couldn't be painted like steel or aluminum parts, since they couldn't be cured in an extremely hot oven. To ensure a high-quality finish, BMW Technik worked with the material suppliers and AKZO Coatings to develop the new Varioflex paint process, which allowed the paint to remain uniformly flexible even on panels which themselves had varying degrees of flexibility. Following application, the two-stage primer and color coats were cured for 30 minutes at a relatively low 186°F before the final coat of clear was applied. Each component received a specific type of clear coat according to the degree of flexibility it required, after which it was dried for an additional 45 minutes at a slightly lower temperature of 176-185°F.

The first recyclable BMW?

Although it was never revealed when the car was new, the body panels were designed to be fully recyclable. "We wanted to be the first to address a big issue of consumer goods and to show a solution," Dr. Bez told me. "This was presented to the VDA [*Verband der Automobilindustrie*, Germany's automotive trade organization] OEM committee, which wanted us to let sleeping dogs lie. The BMW board followed this request, and didn't allow us to announce this innovation."

Today, of course, nearly every part of a BMW can be recycled, and end-of-life directives are included at the start of any vehicle project.

Along with newfound flexibility and recycle-ability, the front bumper contained a novel interpretation of BMW's double-kidney grille, one that drew inspiration from the small kidneys used on the M1 supercar and the Turbo concept of 1972. The kidneys were flanked by wide slots on either side, which ensured adequate cooling air for the radiator and front brakes. The front bumper also held the fog lights and turn signals, which Lagaaij designed as visual extensions

of the glass panels that covered the Bosch headlights. Even though retractable headlights were all the rage in the mid-1980s, Lagaaij never liked them, and in any case they added unwanted air resistance to a car designed for maximum aerodynamic performance.

The car needed downforce at both ends to be effective, but Lagaaij had rejected the idea of a rear wing from the outset. A solution came from racing: BMW was fresh from winning the 1983 Formula One world championship, and its work with Brabham had underscored the importance of a car's floor to its aerodynamic performance. On the Z1, the floor was designed to produce downforce via panels around the engine and gearbox, and the exhaust system's muffler made an equally important contribution. The muffler (**shown on page 30**) used a patented design that gave it the shape of an early F1 rear wing, and it pushed air outward through a wide slit between the rear bumper and the trunk lid.

In January 1986, the Z1 was tested in the Pininfarina wind tunnel in Italy. The low frontal area provided low resistance, and the car displayed an excellent drag coefficient with its top up or down. More cooling air was required in the engine bay, so the necessary modifications were completed by Lutz Janssen's aero and heat management team upon their return to Munich.

Over the next several months, BMW Technik's engineers and designers refined the prototype's performance while fitting the basic equipment needed in every automobile, including heating and ventilation. Wheels are an obvious necessity, and in the case of the Z1 they weren't simply pulled from existing inventory.

Lagaaij wanted something special and distinctive, and he drew a wheel with an odd number of spokes for an eye-catching effect. "Seven spokes irritate the eye at first, then there is a slight unrest, and it is precisely this unrest that creates the appeal that makes this rim so attractive," he told Lewandowski. The wheels were sand-cast in prototype form, then manufactured in aluminum by Pedrini of Italy.

Like the wheels, the cockpit needed to be special. The Z1 got experimental seats from Bertrand-Faure, which featured exceptionally supportive foam inside a plastic shell in body color. The seating position was unusually deep, set between the door sills and a wide tunnel for the catalytic converter and the driveshaft.

Testing and refinement

On July 22, 1986, the BMW board of directors were invited to drive the completed prototype on the roads around Ismaning, just outside Munich. Chairman Eberhard von Kuenheim reportedly liked it, remarking that it would be a good car for his son. Dr. Wolfgang Reitzle, then head of BMW's development division, took issue with an inelegant curve above the door, as well as the height of the side lines, but Lagaaij was already in the process of addressing both issues.

The favorable response meant the project would continue, with BMW Technik's one hundred engineers working with those from series production to refine the car using BMW's supercomputer for mathematical analysis as well as the parent company's testing capabilities. The car was included in the regular rotation for testing in hot and cold weather, at high speed at Nardo in Italy, for drivability and handling at Miramas in France, and on roads in Spain and the Alps.

BMW decided to "leak" news of the prototype to the press, and to let a few journalists in Germany and the UK—including Lewandowski—drive it. Though they weren't allowed to examine its chassis, the journalists loved the car's go-kart handling and roadster bodywork, and their favorable impressions generated considerable interest in the car. Customers began trying to place orders, a good sign for any new car and a strong indication that the roadster was due for a revival.

In the meantime, the other details were being finalized. From Audi, Lagaaij hired Sabine Zemelka and Stefan Stark to work on colors and materials for the Z1's interior and exterior. Since the car was still a concept, not a pre-production model, they tried to anticipate trends that would be *au courant* a few years out, attending design fairs and following the worldwide art scene. They wanted the car to be modern, but not overwhelmingly so. Printed leather and Nubuck brought new touches to the interior,

while a traditional approach to the dashboard and gauges reflected the simplicity and purity of the driving experience.

For the car's exterior, Lagaaij lowered the belt line, which changed the door height and installation depth. The doors would be built by Brose, and the team decided to raise and lower them via an electric motor and toothed belt, with hand operation as a fail-safe. The side windows would go into position automatically.

Even after the change, the sills remained high enough that the car could be driven with the doors retracted, allowing driver and passenger to see the pavement passing by at close range, much as they would on a motorcycle. The car's crash protection was unaffected, and it displayed exemplary safety in crash testing on December 15, 1986.

Three days later, the Z1 was shown to the board of management.

"I presented the Z1 project with a five-minute film, and each of my key people had 45 seconds to present his part. None of the board members could interrupt," Bez told me. "The expectation was that the project would be canceled, but Eberhard von Kuenheim handled it with sovereignty. He asked the head of sales [Dr. Eberhard von Körber] for how much he could sell the car. The answer was DM 80,000—my proposal had been DM 50,000!—with the intention of killing it. Von Kuenheim nodded and said, 'Good price for a limited number of cars. Let's do 5,000 cars. Does anyone object?' After hearing von Kuenheim's opinion, everybody agreed!"

Returning to BMW Technik, Bez delivered the news. "I assembled all my key people to inform them about the decision. Guess the first reaction: Not jubilation, but moaning! Now we have to deliver! That initial reaction was followed by huge satisfaction, and Yes, we can!"

From experiment to production

With that, the project was assigned a number within BMW's official *Entwicklung* series for production vehicles. Since it borrowed so many parts from the E30 3 Series, the Z1 became known internally as E30/Z.

Discussions about translating the prototype into production were followed by the first orders, placed by Bez and Lagaaij. The specialized chassis and other parts precluded production on the regular line in any of BMW's existing factories, but BMW Technik figured that 1-5 cars per day could be built by hand.

"At first, we were looking for a place within Europe that could build in smaller quantities," Bez told Lewandowski, "then BMW AG's Munich factory wanted to do a pilot program in one of its halls, setting up a provisional assembly line for series production cars before they moved to the main hall for large-scale production."

No major investment would be required, and the hall would be ready in 1988. In the meantime, Baur would build the earliest prototypes, followed by the monocoque for series production.

In spring 1987, the Z1 was in the wind tunnel, undergoing final refinements centered on occupant comfort. The aero team wanted to reduce air velocity close to the car's bodywork, to minimize draft on the occupants, and they focused on changes to the A-pillar, the exterior mirrors (mounted about one-third of the way up the pillar rather than at the bottom, as is customary), and the car's rear.

In June 1987, the board decided to show the Z1 at Frankfurt that September, and to take orders if customers wanted to buy it. On August 10, 1987, BMW announced that its hand-built roadster would indeed be offered to the public. The response was immediate, and the Z1 created a sensation even before the Frankfurt show opened. After seeing the Ur-Green prototype on display, several thousand customers placed orders for a car that wouldn't be available for another year, and which would indeed cost DM 80,000, or $44,444. (By the time the car went on sale, the price had escalated to DM 83,500.) The price would include a radio and hi-fi audio system, metallic paint, and leather upholstery, with no real options available beyond a choice of four colors: Ur-Green, Top Red, Dream Black metallic, and Fun Yellow. (Pure Blue and Magic Violet were added in 1991.) Since the plastic bodywork could be removed with ordinary tools

and fasteners, it was suggested that customers could have a second set in another color, which could be changed like a suit of clothes according to the mood of the moment.

Advancing from the prototype stage, the Z1 got the typical detail refinements from BMW: quality assurance, chassis tuning, steering optimization, noise-vibration-and-harshness reduction, acoustic tuning, and temperature stability.

As promised, BMW's specialized production hall was ready by spring 1988, and by June the press fleet was ready, along with 30 cars for the marketing department.

Following the international press launch in Punta Ala, Italy, the Z1 drew near-universal praise as BMW's most fun car to drive in decades. If any complaints were registered, they centered on the engine, which was deemed somewhat ordinary for such a remarkable roadster.

The favorable reviews helped the Z1 attract some 4,000 advance orders before series production began in March 1989. By the time the Z1's run came to an end in June 1991, a total of 8,013 cars had been built. One was used to create the Z1 M, a "beefy racer" from BMW Motorsport that failed to advance beyond the prototype stage.

The Z1 was never sold new in the US, and the vast majority—6,443 cars—were sold in Germany. Of the rest, 445 were sold in Italy, 347 in France, 176 in Belgium, and 153 in Austria. The remainder were sold throughout Europe, with a handful going to Middle Eastern countries, South Africa, Panama, and Japan.

Roadsters are emotional products, and the Z1 inspired more passion than most BMWs. In the fall of 1990, BMW Motorsport responded by offering a Z1 adventure tour in the south of France. For DM 3,500, or $1,842, enthusiasts could drive BMW-provided Z1s around the Paul Ricard circuit as well as public roads, while staying in "smart sport hotels with kindred spirits and in the most exclusive style."

An outsized legacy

By the time the Z1 was delighting enthusiasts, Dr. Ulrich Bez had returned to Porsche; project manager Dr. Klaus Faust would end up shepherding the Z1 through production. Bez would spend four years on the Porsche board of management with responsibility for research, engineering and motorsport; in 1992, he left Porsche for South Korea's Daewoo, where he became head of engineering and auto development. In 2000, he was named CEO of Aston Martin, the British sports car company he led until 2015. Today, Dr. Bez serves on several corporate boards and runs his own consulting firm. Despite his considerable accomplishments, the Z1 holds a special place in his heart.

"The Z1 was my first whole-car project," Bez told me in 2021. "It is still a dream project, and the small team worked passionately and competently together. The experience of designing, engineering, producing, and marketing a whole car was my entrance back to Porsche, and the 993, 968, then the Daewoo Matiz and more than twenty Aston Martin models."

Bez may have moved on from BMW, but he still has his Ur-Green Z1. In March 2021, he registered the car for the first time, with zero miles on the odometer, "to drive around the mountains and down to Provence to pick some flowers from the roadside with the door down!"

Designer Harm Lagaaij would follow Bez back to Porsche, where he'd worked from 1971 to 1977 before being named Ford's chief of design in Cologne. Returning to Porsche from BMW, Lagaaij led the design team in Weissach from 1989 until his retirement in 2004.

While advancing the careers of those who created it, the Z1 did even more to advance the development process within BMW. More publicly, it solidified BMW's image as a maker of technically innovative cars that were also elemental and fun to drive—qualities that offered a crucial contrast to BMW's upmarket sedans of the era.

The Z1 had the further effect of galvanizing interest in the roadster segment, paving the way for the hugely popular Mazda Miata that debuted in 1989. The success of the Miata, in turn, inspired BMW to green-light another roadster, the Z3 we'll examine in the next chapter.

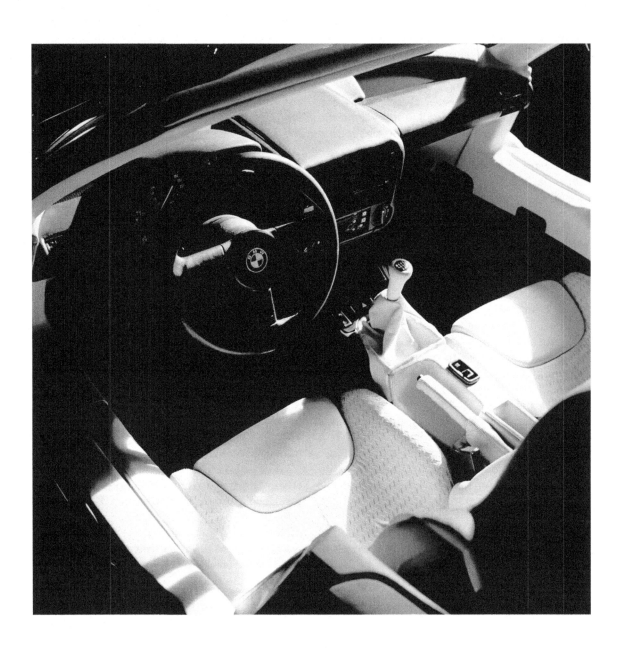

Z2: The Z1's hardtop sibling

While Z1 was still under development, BMW Technik began exploring the possibilities of platform engineering. The goal was to investigate new methods and technologies that would "facilitate a maximally efficient extension of a vehicle concept to additional derivatives."

In other words, BMW Technik wanted to find out how quickly and cost-effectively new body styles could be developed atop a single platform.

In 1988, Technik's engineers built the Z2 coupe atop the Z1's floor pan and chassis. The Z2 retained the Z1's signature drop-down doors beneath its fixed roof, the greenhouse of which was set well within the rear fenders. That design theme that would be repeated a few years later, when BMW transformed the Z3 roadster into the Z3 coupe, and again in the 21st century when the Z4 roadster gained its own coupe counterpart.

Z1 Art Car by AR Penck

BMW's Art Car series began in 1975, when Parisian art dealer and amateur racer Hervé Poulain sourced a 3.0 CSL from BMW Motorsport and commissioned Alexander Calder to paint it. The car raced in the 24 Hours of Le Mans, where it attracted so much favorable publicity that BMW decided to carry on when Poulain suggested that another CSL painted by Frank Stella in 1976, followed by cars from Roy Lichtenstein and Andy Warhol. All were raced at Le Mans.

In 1982, BMW began commissioning artists directly, engaging them to create museum pieces for static display rather than kinetic competition. Seven years later, BMW engaged German artist AR Penck to transform a Z1 into the company's eleventh Art Car. It was a fine choice, as Penck considered the Z1 a work of art even before he applied his signature hieroglyphics to the plastic bodywork. "The product itself is already the expression of the creativity and imagination of its designers and engineers," he was quoted in *BMW Art Cars*, a 2014 retrospective. "And this was interesting to me: to create art on the surface of a three-dimensional object."

Like the other artists chosen to create BMW's Art Cars, Penck was already well established in his field. A native of Dresden, he was born Ralf Winkler in 1939. He began painting and sculpting while a teenager, but he was refused admission to art schools in Communist-controlled East Germany and remained largely self-taught. Working as a mailman or a night watchman, among other jobs, Penck (his pseudonym since 1969) studied not just art but mathematics, physics, and music, playing free jazz (drums) while developing his signature stick figures and symbols. "I wanted to capture man's primal fears, from the very beginning until our own time."

His style was so offensive to the authorities—lying far afield from the state's preferred Social Realism—that Penck was stripped of his East German citizenship in 1980 even though he was already an internationally recognized artist. He left East Germany first for Cologne, then

London. In 1988, Penck became a professor of painting at the Academy of Arts in Düsseldorf, and in 1989 he was commissioned by BMW to paint the Z1. Penck agreed to forego his fee if the car could make its debut in Moscow, a location he believed would irritate the East German authorities.

Penck was scheduled to paint the last Z1 built, which would be completed in 1991. Before that could happen, the Berlin Wall fell, and the East German state collapsed. Instead of Moscow, the AR Penck Art Car debuted in Dresden, the home from which he had been involuntarily exiled.

About his Art Car, Penck said, "The point of an art work, first of all, is not what is represented, but rather that it is represented and how it is represented. That's what constitutes a style. It's what is intrinsic to painting: proportion, distance, rhythm, form, relationship between forms, etc. An artwork is nothing more than a state of being. Either it is a reproduced state of being, or it is an invented state of being. It depends."

AR Penck died in 2017 in Zurich, age 77.

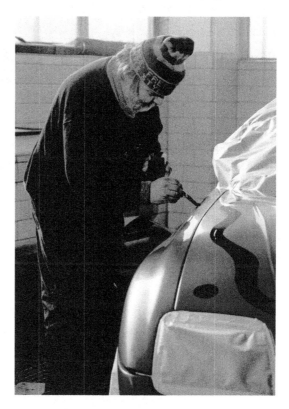

E36/7 Z3 roadster
From Miata rival to M-car

On February 9, 1989, Mazda debuted its new MX-5 Miata roadster at the Chicago auto show. Like the Z1 at Frankfurt, the Miata was an overnight sensation, attracting high praise and a flurry of advance orders. Production began in April, and by early June it had outstripped total Z1 production. By the end of the year, Mazda had built 45,2366 of the diminutive roadsters, and in 1990 it built 95,640 more.

What made the Miata so popular? Let's look at the spec sheet. The car was small, with a curb weight of just 2,210 pounds. Beneath its hood, the Miata was powered a 1.6-liter four-cylinder engine with a lively 116 horsepower at 6,500 rpm and 100 pound-feet at 5,500 rpm. A five-speed manual was the only transmission, delivering power to the rear wheels. Zero-to-60 mph acceleration was a modest but acceptable 9.2 seconds, top speed 116 mph.

The total package added up to far more than what was on the spec sheet. Put simply, the Miata succeeded because it combined the fun of a classic English sports car with the reliability of a Japanese compact.

As *Car and Driver*'s Arthur St. Antoine wrote in 1989: "The Miata fairly glows with the automotive ideals that this magazine holds dear—exciting looks, fun to drive, sensible ergonomics, quality construction, fun to drive, refined mechanicals, affordable price, and—did we forget to mention?—fun to drive. The Miata is also commendable for what it doesn't deliver—namely, large oil stains on your garage floor and roadside breakdowns."

That description could have applied just as easily to the Z1, of course, but far fewer enthusiasts—and only a handful in the US—were able to experience the BMW roadster. Rather than a hand-built technology showcase, the Miata was a conventional but well-engineered car. With a base price of just $13,800, it was also affordable, which the Z1 most definitely was not.

The Z1 was always perceived as a niche product, but the Miata's mainstream success rippled through the auto industry. Nearly every manufacturer scrambled to come up with a competing roadster of its own.

Naturally, BMW was among them.

Photo courtesy Joji Nagashima, sketch courtesy BMW Design

Designing BMW's "Fun Car"

If the Z1 began as an exploration of a simple concept, that of "freedom on four wheels," its successor began in 1989 as a study of something even more basic: fun.

"'Fun Car' was a minor sketch assignment made up just to keep designers busy," Joji Nagashima told me in 2021. Then a 33-year-old designer at BMW in Munich, he's seen more recently in the photo opposite, below. "The car wasn't defined as a roadster or a sports car. It could be anything. I started sketching something like a beach buggy, just because it looked 'fun,' though in the series of sketches I tried one roadster that looked a bit like a 328, a retro design."

Inspired by Nagashima's keen sense of BMW history, it represented a marked departure from Harm Lagaaij's Z1. "The Z1 was certainly an interesting car, but I felt it wasn't 'BMW' enough, with regard to shape, emotion, or tradition. In that sense, the Z3 was my antithesis to the Z1," Nagashima told me. "I don't think a roadster can be a modern type of car in any case. It's uncomfortable over 130 km/h (80 mph), and you can't even listen to the radio at 80 km/h (50 mph). Once you open the top, there's no such thing as aerodynamics, because aerodynamic efficiency is so far behind today's standard."

Given that the Z1's smooth, unadorned exterior had been considered too "Japanese" for some BMW purists, it's ironic that a designer born in Tokyo would take BMW back to its roots. Perhaps, but Nagashima is a lifelong enthusiast of automotive history who began drawing cars while still in kindergarten. He earned his undergraduate degree in Craft and Industrial Design from Tokyo's Musashino Art University, then completed a Master's in Industrial Design at Wayne State University in Michigan. In 1980, Nagashima took his first design job at Opel in Rüsselsheim, Germany; six years later, he moved to Renault.

In 1988, Nagashima joined the BMW design studio, working in Exterior Design under Klaus Kapitza—one of two Exterior Design studio chiefs at the time, the other being Boyke Boyer—and Claus Luthe, head of BMW Design since 1976.

The "Fun Car" sketches were among Nagashima's earliest in Munich. After they were completed, the project went dormant until veteran designer Manfred Rennen needed something on which his trainee modelers could practice. Rennen asked Nagashima and another designer, Jan Hettler, to provide the modelers with something to work up in clay, giving them no further instruction.

"Jan and I decided to do a roadster split model, a clay model with different designs on each side, on an imaginary short-wheelbase E36 package," Nagashima said. "When we finished, Luthe decided to eliminate one side, and to bounce my design to the other side to complete the model. At that time, there was another two-seat convertible presentation by BMW Technik, and Luthe wanted to show them my model. The reaction was pretty good, but this was still an in-house research presentation that had nothing to do with production."

Input from the motorcycle side

Perhaps, but documentation in the BMW Design Archive shows that Nagashima's Fun Car model was actually one of five presented for consideration. Two of the others were from BMW Technik, and another was a "buggy" from BMW Motorsport. None of those three would advance beyond the modeling stage, while Nagashima's was selected for further development with more differentiation to a cabriolet. The fifth, built by BMW Motorrad [Motorcycles], would be built as a prototype by the division led by Dr. Burkhard Göschel.

"As the roadster project started, BMW's head of strategic planning, Dr. Peter-Alexander Wacker, asked me to make a roadster concept," Dr. Göschel told me in 2021. "His idea was that motorcycles would be closer to a roadster concept than BMW's car division."

In selecting Göschel for the project, Wacker had made an inspired choice. Born in 1945, Göschel was a second-generation enthusiast of high-performance automobiles. He grew up near Stuttgart, where his father had worked for Mercedes during World War II. At Mercedes, the elder Göschel developed the world's first direct-

injection two-stroke engine, a technology he applied to Gutbrod automobiles after the war. Gutbrod introduced its fuel-injected automobile engine in 1953, three years before Mercedes would do the same. Shortly thereafter, the elder Göschel returned to Mercedes, where he'd engineer the company's Formula One engines.

After giving medical school a brief try, Göschel (at far right in the 2002 photo opposite, with BMW's post-1992 design chief Chris Bangle at left) followed his father into engineering. He completed his degree at the Technical University of Munich in 1971, then spent four years as a research engineer while studying for his doctorate at Stuttgart University. Göschel finished his studies in 1976, then worked on engine pre-development at Daimler for two years before taking a similar post at BMW.

Göschel worked in the engine department until 1989, when he was named head of motorcycle development. In that role, he developed the oil-cooled cylinder head that allowed BMW to retain its traditional opposed twin-cylinder Boxer engine while meeting the noise and emissions requirements that nearly relegated it to history.

That ability to blend tradition with innovation was undoubtedly what brought Göschel to the fore when it was time to develop a new BMW roadster. Working with Strategic Planning's Ralph Speth—later CEO of Jaguar/Land Rover—and motorcycle designer Martin Longmore, Göschel came up with a vehicle that borrowed its four-cylinder engine and chassis parts from the E30 3 Series. In other respects, it was entirely unconventional. "It was a basic roadster with detachable door side panels and a detachable trunk cover," Göschel said. "You could have used it as a roadster pickup!"

Motorrad's project had a strong champion in Dr. Reitzle, said Nagashima. "He was a car guy, and I could feel that he was really excited about the idea of a lightweight sports car."

Nagashima continued to explore the possibilities for a BMW roadster, and one of his 1991 sketches is shown on the previous spread. "I was still wondering how much 328-ness should be reflected on the production car," Nagashima told me in 2021. "I tried a lot of sketches, and this was the wildest and most retro looking one. I thought this was too extreme, not appropriate for a mainstream sports car. For me, production car design is always about how not to go too far."

By early 1992, the success of the Miata had bolstered the business case for a new BMW roadster, and Reitzle put forth three models—including the Motorrad proposal and Nagashima's Fun Car—for consideration by the full BMW board of management.

"I still remember the day Reitzle presented the model," Nagashima says. "By that time, Claus Luthe had resigned [as head of BMW Design] and Hans Braun was interim design chief—Chris Bangle was not yet with us. It was somewhat late, around 6 p.m. or so. Suddenly, the door opened, and an excited Reitzle rushed in, telling me in English, 'Your car will be running on the road!'"

Equally exciting, the car designated internally as the E36/7—being the seventh body-style derivative of the E36 3 Series—would be developed for production by Dr. Göschel. The motorcycle division's project had been deemed second-best, but the board apparently liked the creativity and passion it displayed.

So did Nagashima. "[Göschel] had a huge head of curly hair, like a hippie, and he was known as a crazy driver," says Nagashima. "I liked him a lot."

Keeping it simple...and affordable

Nagashima and Göschel—plus interior designer Michael Ninic—would have more enthusiasm than budget with which to realize their vision. Where the Z1 was created with few limitations and cutting-edge technology, the new roadster would be extremely cost-constrained, sourcing as many parts as possible from the then-new E36 3 Series.

"I was told to do the car as a 'first BMW,' not as a serious sports car," Nagashima told me. "The car was supposed to be a compact, fun-to-drive city commuter for DM 40,000 ($25,641)."

That price precluded a motorized top, and it necessitated a few other compromises,

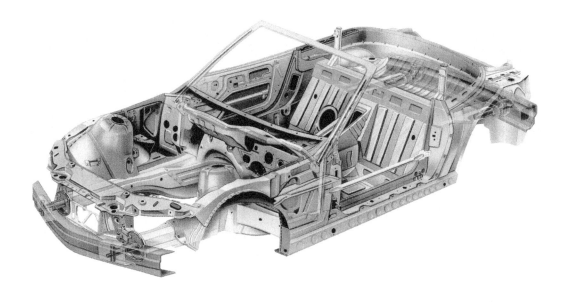

Images courtesy BMW Archive

including the use of several components from the previous-generation E30 3 Series and other parts borrowed directly from the E36. "I wasn't even allowed to change the standard E36 seat rails to lower the head clearance," Nagashima says. "We started the clay model before the head hard point was definitively determined. When we got the finalized point, the lower body was almost done and we couldn't start anything over. We tried every possible trick, though the soft top always looked 25mm (1.0 inch) too tall."

Dr. Göschel received the same brief on the engineering side. "The approach was unchanged from that of BMW motorcycles. It should be a fun-to-drive, entry-level BMW. Cost should be kept low, since it's only for fun, and we needed to make it simple and easy to handle."

Rather than a six-cylinder engine, the lightweight Z3 would be powered by the 1,895cc M44 four-cylinder. With four valves per cylinder, the M44 delivered 138 horsepower at 6,000 rpm and 133 pound-feet at 4,300 rpm. The engine was paired with a five-speed Getrag Type C manual transmission or an optional four-speed THM R1 automatic. The latter offered three shift modes: Economy, Sport, and Manual.

The new roadster's chassis would be based on that of the E36 3 Series, but with its wheelbase shortened by a full ten inches to 96.3 inches. That in itself would give the car agile handling in the twisties, especially when the car got its cornering instructions through a steering rack with a 13.9:1 ratio that was much more direct than the 3 Series' 16.8:1.

Like the Z1, the new roadster borrowed its MacPherson strut front suspension from the current 3 Series, which had received improved geometry and caster angle in its evolution from E30 to E36.

Where the rear suspension was concerned, the new roadster took a step backwards, returning to the E30's semi-trailing arm setup rather than the multilink Z-axle developed for the Z1 and incorporated on the then-new E36. Developed for the 1957 600 microcar, the semi-trailing arm rear axle was said to be a better fit in the roadster's limited space. It

was certainly cost-effective; as chassis engineer Heinz Krusche told me in 2009, "The primary instruction we got was, 'Keep it cheap!'"

Regardless of why it was chosen, the semi-trailing arms gave the roadster less mechanical grip than the Z-axle would have provided, resulting in lively handling that was perfectly in keeping with the car's mission. "Using the E30 suspension/axle concept made the Z3 a lot of fun to drive," Göschel said.

The new roadster's mechanical connection to the 3 Series gave the car its development code, E36/7, as well as its model name. Having re-established its roadster line with the Z1, BMW decided to designate all of its roadsters with the letter Z even though they were no longer developed at BMW Technik, aka ZT. The nomenclature allowed the new roadster to borrow a little of the Z1's glamour, while bringing it within BMW's mainstream naming convention.

Making its debut as the Z3 1.9, the roadster was pretty tame in its original incarnation. The M44 four-cylinder's 138 horsepower marked a significant upgrade over the Miata's 116 horsepower, but the advantage was negated by an increase in weight. At 2,690 pounds (manual transmission), the Z3 outweighed the 2,210-pound Miata by 480 pounds. As a result, the two cars ended up virtually tied in the zero-to-60 mph dash, the Z3 needing 9.1 seconds to reach that benchmark while the Miata took 9.0. (With the optional automatic, the Z3 weighed 2,767 pounds and hit 60 mph in 9.7 seconds.)

The Z3 was more expensive than the Miata, too. In November 1995, the Z3 1.9 had a base price of $28,750 to the Miata's $13,800.

A BMW made in the US

In a stroke of product-placement genius, the Z3 made its first public appearance not at an auto show, but in a James Bond movie: Goldeneye saw Agent 007 swap his customary Aston Martin for a blue Z3. Its appearance on-screen was brief, but it created a tidal wave of anticipation, and plenty of advance orders, some of which were placed through the Neiman Marcus Christmas '95 catalog.

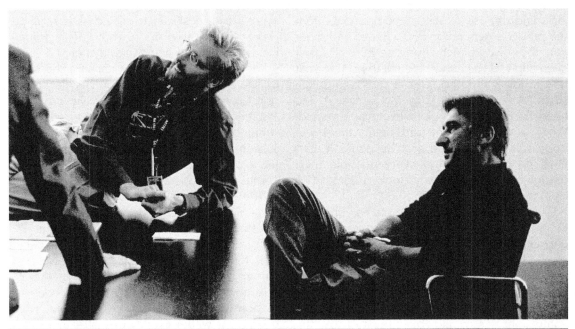

Bangle/Ninic photo courtesy BMW Design,
interior photo courtesy BMW Archive

Shortly after the holiday, in early January 1996, the Z3 made its official debut at the Detroit auto show. Like the Miata, the Z3 was first shown in the US rather than in its parent company's home market. For Mazda, showing the car first in Chicago was a nod toward the car's origins in Southern California. For BMW, it was an acknowledgment that the Z3 would be the first BMW built exclusively in the US.

"During the development phase, BMW decided that the Z3 should go to the new factory to be built in Spartanburg, South Carolina," Dr. Göschel said. "So I got the whole responsibility of developing the car, setting up production, creating a totally new supply base, and integrating it into BMW."

The US was one of BMW's most important markets worldwide, which itself made a strong case for expanding the production network into this country. In addition, producing cars in the US would act as a hedge against the currency fluctuations that had hampered trade with Germany for more than two decades. Having spent the postwar period trading at roughly four *Deutschmarks* to the dollar, the *Deutschmark* began rising sharply in value in 1970. Exchange rates were volatile thereafter, and by 1995 the value of the dollar had fallen to just DM 1.43. Building cars in Spartanburg—with cheaper, non-union US labor, and with parts purchased from suppliers located nearby—allowed BMW to stabilize pricing for US customers.

It also galvanized brand loyalty, particularly after BMW Manufacturing added its Zentrum reception hall on the factory grounds. Built at the urging of BMW of North America CEO Dr. Helmut Panke, the Zentrum highlighted BMW's heritage by displaying vintage automobiles and motorcycles, and it offered enthusiasts a place to gather for meetings and events.

In 1997, a group led by Amy and Wayne Lester used the burgeoning internet forums to organize the first Z3 Homecoming at Spartanburg. Expected to draw a handful of local Z3 owners, the Z3 Homecoming ended up drawing several hundred from much farther afield. Over its twelve-year run, the Homecoming brought thousands of enthusiasts from all over the continent to Spartanburg.

Not all car owners are inclined to visit the factories where their cars are made, but those who bought Z3s became emotionally attached to a degree that was rare even among BMW enthusiasts.

History-minded BMW enthusiasts loved its resemblance to the classic 328, but Nagashima's fun-loving exterior was more than just retro. With its friendly face, the Z3 attracted plenty of newcomers to the BMW brand, people who might not have been interested in a more serious-looking sports car like an M3.

The Z3 was given a similarly inviting design by Michael Ninic (**seen seated in the photo opposite, with Chris Bangle on the table**), a graduate of Munich's Industrial Design Academy who began his career at Audi in 1980. After two years in Ingolstadt, Ninic went to Porsche Design before joining BMW's interior design department at BMW in 1986.

Ninic's interior was clean and basic, with nothing extraneous to clutter the purity of the roadster experience. Although its dimensions made occupants a little cramped, it had perfect ergonomics for the task of driving. Simply put, it was a fun place to be, and it added to the affection the Z3 engendered among its owners…and the automotive press.

A "nifty little sports car"

"This is one nifty little sports car," wrote Tony Swan in *Car and Driver* in 1996. "With its firm suspension, quick steering and meaty 16-in. tires, the Z3 can change directions quicker than a politician and grips the road in high speed corners like a race car. The only surprise that emerged was just how high this car's absolute cornering limits are. There's more grip here than most of us will ever use, a nice reserve for emergency maneuvers and a big plus for hard braking.

"Engine performance is generally in step with the rest of the Z3's dynamic traits. Acceleration falls short of eyeball-flattening territory, but it's brisk, about 8 seconds or so to 60 mph, and midrange response is satisfying. Top speed is electronically limited to 116 mph. For those who want more, a more potent Z3, probably

equipped with the 328's 190-hp 6-cyl. engine, is about a year down the road."

Swan concluded by addressing the matter of cost, and whether the Z3 was worth the price premium over a comparable Miata: "A terrific sports car in its own right, the Miata offers similar performance. And even though a Miata equipped up to the level of a standard Z3 costs about $23,000, that's still a significant price disparity.

"However, the Z3 is a better car—roomier, quieter, more substantial and built to a slightly higher standard. The Z3 conveys a stronger sense of solidity than the Miata, and we'll be surprised if it falls prey to the buzzes, squeaks and rattles that show up in a lot of other convertibles. We think anyone who steps up to the Z3's higher price will never regret it."

The six-cylinder Z3 to which Swan referred was indeed on the way, and enthusiasts wouldn't have long to wait. The Z3 2.8 (opposite, below) arrived in late 1996, designated as a model year 1997 vehicle. Along with a 2,793cc M52 inline six with 189 horsepower and 203 pound-feet, the Z3 2.8 had its rear track widened by 2.6 inches. That necessitated new bodywork, primarily the wider rear fenders and new front spoiler designed by Andreas Zapatinas.

The Z3 2.8 also got a limited-slip differential, ASC+T traction control, ventilated brake discs, leather upholstery, and wood trim—all of which took the Z3 2.8 considerably upmarket with respect to its four-cylinder counterpart. Its $35,900 price reflected those upgrades, and it also bought a much faster car: The Z3 2.8 ran the zero-to-60 mph dash in just 6.3 seconds, nearly three seconds quicker than the four-cylinder 1.9.

Throughout its seven-year production run, the Z3 received a series of upgrades. Most notably, ASC+T traction control became standard for 1997, while rollover protection was added for 1998 along with new Sport and Premium Package options.

When BMW of North America adopted an all-six-cylinder strategy for 1999, the Z3 1.9 was replaced by the Z3 2.3 as the base model. The new model was powered by the 2,494cc M52TU six, with variable timing (VANOS) on both camshafts and Siemens MS 42 engine management. With 170 horsepower at 5,500 rpm and 181 pound-feet at 3,500 rpm, zero-to-60 improved to 6.8 seconds.

In 2001, the M52TU was superseded by the higher-revving M54. The base Z3 became the Z3 2.5i, powered by the 2,494cc M54 with 184 horsepower at 6,000 rpm and 175 pound-feet at 3,500 rpm, delivered through a Getrag Type B five-speed manual. Zero-to-60 mph acceleration was a little slower at 7.1 seconds, but the M54 felt zingier, and more fun to run to redline.

The Z3 2.8, meanwhile, was replaced by the Z3 3.0i, in which the 2,979cc M54 delivered 225 horsepower at 5,900 rpm and 214 pound-feet at 3,500 rpm. Acceleration was a brisk 5.9 seconds from zero to 60 mph with the standard ZF Type C five-speed manual transmission. A GM-built five-speed Steptronic automatic was available on both models, which were offered through the 2002 model year.

By the end of the Z3's production run, BMW had sold 113,712 examples in the US, and 128,605 in Europe. Worldwide production totaled 247,298 units, making the Z3 a resounding success even if its numbers would never rival those of the Miata. For a niche manufacturer like BMW, the car was a huge hit, and it ensured that roadsters would have a place in the lineup for decades to come.

So did its designer, who remains at BMW to this day. Joji Nagashima followed his work on the Z3 by designing the exterior of the E39 5 Series and E90 3 Series.

M roadster: Too much is never enough!

Even in standard form, the six-cylinder Z3s had plenty of performance for everyday use, or for a spirited drive on a twisty mountain road. That doesn't mean that enthusiasts weren't clamoring for more, or that engineers like Dr. Burkhard Göschel would leave well enough alone.

By 1993, Göschel had been put in charge of "Special Vehicles." That would come to include several new BMW models, the first of which was a high-performance version of the Z3 roadster.

BMW's M brand was on a roll, having just introduced the E36 M3 with the ultra-exotic S50 six-cylinder engine under its hood. That car wouldn't come to the US, though a less-expensive version was in the works thanks to some behind-the-scenes finagling by Motorsport manager Karl-Heinz Kalbfell and BMW of North America's Erik Wensberg, bolstered by a letter-writing campaign from members of the BMW Car Club of America.

BMW M was eager to expand its brand beyond the M3 and M5, and the Z3 was an obvious target for M-ification. Technically, however, the short-wheelbase roadster presented a few challenges in high-horsepower form.

"Chassis flex was a real concern," said Wensberg in 2021. "There were tire issues, as well as concern with the short wheelbase with all the power the engines were bringing."

Nonetheless, the car went ahead, and the minimally-named M roadster was displayed at the Geneva auto salon in March 1996— even before the Z3 2.8 became available.

The M roadster had been designed by Marcus Syring, who'd become the youngest member of the BMW Motorsport design team in 1991. Syring was inspired by the powerful shape of the AC Cobra, and it was obvious at a glance that he had penned a far more muscular Z3: Its front air dam was deeply sculpted to produce downforce, its fog lights were replaced by brake ducts, and its rear bumper featured cutouts for four exhaust pipes rather than two. Its front flanks wore chrome-trimmed "gills" in place of the Z3's body-colored air vents, recalling those on the 507 roadster of the 1950s.

Inside, the M roadster was even more distinctive, with two-tone leather upholstery and nostalgic chrome trim around the instruments, among other touches. All of these changes were made not at BMW Design in Munich but by designers at BMW M in Garching, which then enjoyed significant autonomy from the main design department.

The M roadster's ride height was 1.1 inches lower than the Z3's, while its wheel tracks were wider by 0.4 inches at both axles. The car rode on stiffer springs coupled with firmer dampers, its front suspension geometry was modified for better high-speed stability, and its rear trailing arms were strengthened along with the subframe and anti-roll bars. The M roadster got the M3's larger disc brakes, set behind stylish 17-inch wheels exclusive to the model.

All of those mods were meant to contain the abundant power from 3.2-liter S50 engine, which featured an iron block with an aluminum cylinder head, 11.3:1 compression, six individual throttle bodies, Double VANOS variable valve timing, advanced BMW/Siemens MSS50 engine management, lightweight pistons, a dual-mass flywheel, and more. This exotic powerplant delivered 321 horsepower (DIN) at 7,400 rpm and 258 pound feet at 3,250 rpm—a lot of power for a car with a 96-3-inch wheelbase. A ZF Type C five-speed manual was the only transmission offered, with a limited-slip differential as the only form of traction control.

Production of the Euro-spec M roadster (E36/7S) began in Spartanburg in September 1996, but the car didn't have its formal press launch until March 1997. Testing the car on the Grand Prix circuit at Jerez in Spain, journalists fell hard for this diminutive powerhouse, praising not only its power but its exciting handling.

Their high marks raised expectations among US enthusiasts, who had to wait until February 1998 to take delivery of the first Z3 M roadsters in this market. As with the E36 M3, the US-spec M roadster would be equipped with a more modest and less expensive engine than its European counterpart: the S52B32US shared with the US-spec E36 M3, which delivered 240 horsepower (SAE) at 6,000 rpm and 236 pound

feet at 3,800 rpm.

Performance was a tamed considerably, but the M roadster was well received in this market nonetheless. BMW of North America sold 8,938 examples of the S52-powered M roadster from 1998 through 2000. That was nearly double the 4,475 S50-powered M roadsters sold in Europe and Great Britain from 1996 to 2000, and it reflected the increasing importance of the North American market to BMW's high-performance ambitions. (It also reflected the US car's more affordable price: $42,200 against the DM 91,500 ($51,989) commanded by the car in Germany.

For 2001, the M division had a new six-cylinder engine, and the M roadster became even more enticing in both Europe and the US.

An evolution of the Euro-spec S50, the S54 (opposite, below) featured a number of detail improvements, including a displacement increase to 3,246cc, 11.5:1 compression, Double VANOS, low-mass rocker arms, MSS 54 engine management, and a scavenging oil pump that ensured adequate oil pressure under high-g cornering. Output rose to 325 hp (DIN) at 7,400 rpm and 258 pound-feet at 4,900 rpm, with the US version registering 315 horsepower and 251 pound-feet (SAE).

The new engine was available for only a brief period at the end of the Z3's run—from February 2001 through May 2002—but BMW of North America sold 1,565 examples of the S54-powered M roadster despite a price hike to $46,635. Underscoring the enthusiasm of North American customers for BMW's most exciting vehicles, that figure represented more than *four times* the number (344) of S54-powered M roadsters sold in Europe and Great Britain.

Worldwide, BMW sold 15,322 examples of the M roadster, certainly a success for a highly-specialized, high-performance sports car.

E36/8 Z3 M coupe
Dr. Göschel's monster

In September 1997, BMW unveiled a totally unexpected vehicle at the Frankfurt auto show. With a fixed roof atop a Z3 body, the M coupe looked decidedly odd, and it polarized show goers and media alike.

Identified as the M coupe, the car had been developed by Dr. Burkhard Göschel's Special Vehicles division, working independently of any direction from the board. This particular Special Vehicle aimed to address the inherent shortcoming of the Z3 roadster, or any open car: its lack of chassis rigidity.

Even in its earliest incarnation, the Z3 was fun to drive, and the short-wheelbase platform certainly had plenty of potential. Try to feed too much power through its rear wheels, however, and the flexible chassis would tie itself in knots trying to harness it. To Dr. Göschel, the solution was simple: Put a fixed roof on the roadster, and turn it into a two-seat coupe.

Nagashima had a similar idea. "After the first standard version was finished, I proposed three conversions in sketch form: a coupe, a shooting brake, and a low-roof speedster, like Porsche's. However, I do not know if these proposals had any influence at M GmbH. They had their studio

in a separate location at that time."

Göschel says that his team was, in fact, aware of Nagashima's sketches. "We worked closely together, and we knew everything! The coupe version was the most exciting, and very easy to realize."

In its final form, the M coupe's design is attributed to Marcus Syring, then a young designer at BMW Motorsport. As such, he'd been allowed to enter the competition to turn the Z3 roadster into a coupe, and his design won the day. Given that Syring had spent his childhood using modeling clay to transform his Matchbox sedans into GTs, it was no wonder he had a strong sense of how the Z3 could be turned into a hardtop.

After Syring's model was mocked up in clay, fabricators at BMW M welded a steel roof onto the six-cylinder version of the Z3 roadster. As it had on the Z2 concept of 1988, the greenhouse sat well within the wide rear fenders, giving the coupe a quirky but aggressive look.

Along with Göschel, one of the car's early advocates was Dr. Helmut Panke, then serving as head of the Group Planning Division that determined BMW's product strategy. "He loved that car," said BMW's then-design chief Chris Bangle in 2021. "He wanted that car, and he was extremely active about getting it, and cars like it, in front of the board."

R&D chief Dr. Wolfgang Reitzle liked it, too. He presented it to the full board and representatives from BMW's sales organization atop the Zugspitze, Germany's highest mountain.

"The board was against it, but Gabriele Falco, head of sales for Europe, coming from Italy, told the board, 'You can't understand this car with your brain. You have to feel it with your heart.' That was somehow understood as a decision, at least by me!" Göschel said.

Perhaps it was, but the car wouldn't get the green light until BMW of North America agreed to sell it. As the world's largest market for M cars, North America would be crucial to the coupe's success.

"None of us thought much of the look of the car, especially in profile," said Erik Wensberg. "It looked too awkward to be widely appealing, and we saw it as a niche car almost immediately. We already had too much experience with pipe fillers, where you sell 2,500 like a house on fire, and then once all the crazy enthusiasts have bought one the car just dies on the market and you have to incentivize the hell out of the rest of them just to get rid of them. I know it's now sacrilege, but that's what happened in the last years of the E30 M3. It kills the image and exclusivity you've been desperately trying to cultivate."

Wary of seeing coupe sales stall on dealer lots, Wensberg resisted.

"We low-balled the volumes to Munich almost immediately, and then told them we didn't really want the car at all. They pushed back on that, as they needed our market to support the entire project," he said. "Then we told them that if we had to take the car, we only wanted the M version, which they pushed back on as well for the same reason."

Eventually, all parties reached an agreement, and Göschel's Z3 coupe got the green light on

one condition: that the car would cost next to nothing to develop. That meant using as many parts as possible from the existing roadster, and not only its drivetrain and suspension. That's why the E36/8 coupe uses the same interior as the roadster, for the most part, and even the same bodywork from bumper to bumper, including the A-pillar.

Only the roof and tailgate are exclusive to the coupe. The roof ended up being slightly taller than the roadster's convertible top, which in turn required taller side windows that the shallow doors can't quite contain. When fully retracted, the windows stick up slightly from the top of the door, precluding resting one's arm on the door while driving.

Like the M roadster, the M coupe would launch in Europe with the 3.2-liter S50 six, which delivered 321 hp (DIN) at 7,400 rpm and 258 pound-feet at 3,250 rpm to the rear wheels. Compared to the standard Z3, the M coupe featured the same chassis mods as the M roadster: 0.4-inch wider wheel tracks front and rear, a 1.1-inch lower ride height, revised front suspension geometry, stiffer springs and dampers, larger-diameter anti-roll bars, stronger trailing arms, and a reinforced rear subframe.

Where the car's handling was concerned, the fixed roof had a dramatic effect, making the coupe body 2.6 times stiffer than the roadster. Where the Z3 roadster had torsional stiffness rated at 5,600 Newton meters for one degree of twist, the Z3 coupe required 16,400 Newton-meters for one degree of twist. That made it as stiff as the E46 3 Series sedan, and put it right on par with a Porsche 996. Its dynamic measurement was equally impressive, checking in at 29.2 Hertz against the E46's 29.8 Hertz; by comparison, the Z3 M roadster registered a dynamic rating of 18.4 Hertz.

Although it added plenty of stiffness, the roof added only 55 pounds to the Z3's curb weight. The M coupe tipped the scales at 3,025 pounds to the M roadster's 2,970, and it scooted from zero to 62 mph in an identical 5.4 seconds. It didn't cost much more, either, with a base price set at DM 95,000 ($53,977) to the roadster's DM 91,500 ($51,989). Few options were available

beyond a power sunroof, in keeping with the M coupe's mission.

"These cars were made for driving, with no navigation systems or such stuff!" Göschel said.

On the 'Ring, and beyond

Like all true driver's cars, the M coupe faced its sternest test on the Nürburgring. To the surprise of everyone except Dr. Göschel—and Hans Stuck and Jo Winkelhock, who fine-tuned the car's chassis at the 'Ring—the M coupe turned a lap three seconds faster than the 911. "The Porsche guys thought they were the kings of the Nürburgring," said Göschel in 1998, "but now we are as fast or faster than the 911 on the long Nordschleife, with an 8 minute, 27 second lap where the 911 needs 8 minutes, 30 seconds."

That doesn't sound too impressive by today's standards, but it was downright fast for the late 1990s, especially for a car built atop the modest Z3 platform. That time was set by the exotic Euro-spec version, of course, but the car we'd get in the US was no slouch, either.

As with the M3 and M roadster, Americans would get M coupes powered not by the S50 but by the less-exotic and less expensive S52B32US six. Delivering 240 horsepower at 6,000 rpm and 225 pound-feet at 3,800 rpm, the engine wasn't as rev-happy as the Euro S50, but the car's acceleration didn't suffer much in the stop light Grand Prix. As tested by *Road & Track*, it reached 60 mph in 5.5 seconds. The magazine noted that the engine produced a lot of torque for such a small coupe, "so careful throttle modulation is needed to keep the rear from losing grip."

Master it, and you'd be driving a car that *Bimmer* magazine called "a true enthusiast's dream. The M coupe just flat hunkers down and rewards well-timed inputs on the road."

As it had in the M3 and M roadster, the S52 engine kept the M coupe's US price to a very reasonable $41,800—slightly lower than that of its roadster counterpart, and well below the car's price in Germany. Even so, American enthusiasts longed for the Euro-spec car's high-revving engine, and they finally got it in 2001, when the M coupe was offered with the new

S54 six introduced in the E46 M3.

The Z3's shorter wheelbase required a shorter exhaust system, and bearing problems in early S54s saw redline reduced from 8,000 rpm to 7,800 rpm. Those factors combined for slightly reduced power compared to the S54's output in the M3: Horsepower dropped from 333 to 315 at 7,400 rpm, torque from 262 to 251 pound-feet at 4,900 rpm. Under real-world driving conditions, the difference was scarcely noticeable. With the new engine—and traction control standard since 1999—the M coupe could hit 60 mph in 5.0 seconds flat. Its real advantage, of course, was in high-rpm running, increasing time-in-gear on a twisty road or race course. However it was quantified, the S54 engine certainly justified the modest price increase; at $45,635 including destination charges, the M coupe was the high-performance bargain of 2001.

No matter which engine was under its hood, the M coupe embodied all the "wildness" for which Dr. Göschel was known, and it became indelibly associated with the enthusiastic engineer. It also inspired almost fanatical devotion from BMW purists who wanted a stripped-down driver's car rather than a near-luxury GT.

As one might expect, and as Erik Wensberg knew, such purists were few in number.

In Europe and Great Britain, BMW sold 2,999 S50-powered M coupes from 1998 to 2000, followed by 434 S54-powered examples in 2001 and 2002.

In the US, customers snapped up 2,180 of the S52-powered cars from 1998 to 2000, then another 678 S54-powered M coupes in 2001 and 2002. (Like the M roadsters, all M coupes were built in the US, at Spartanburg.)

Two decades later, the latter cars especially are highly prized among enthusiasts, trading at more than twice what they commanded new.

Z3 coupe: Hard top, lower price

For those who wanted the structural rigidity of a hardtop at a lower price, BMW offered a non-M version known simply as the Z3 coupe (**opposite**). But for the fixed roof and tailgate/cargo bay, the Z3 coupe was identical to its roadster sibling.

Introduced as a 1997 model, the M52TU-powered Z3 2.8 coupe sold for $36,200 in the US. In 2001, it was superseded by the Z3 3.0i coupe with the 225-horsepower M54 engine and a slightly higher $37,700 price tag.

Even without the M treatment, both Z3 coupes offered stirring performance, and the cars were well received by the automotive press. "At the end of the day, even for a die-hard enthusiast, the Z3 2.8 is fast enough, sharp enough, and engaging enough to be an immensely satisfying drive. It's also a fair chunk cheaper," declared *Bimmer* magazine in 1998. "It's a practical everyday car that puts a thrill into the daily commute. It is dynamically coherent in a way alien to many modern cars. To truly understand this car, you have to drive it. Hard."

By the end of the Z3 coupe's production run in 2002, the assembly line at Spartanburg had churned out 11,524 examples, not quite double the 6,291 M coupes built during the same time frame.

E52 Z8

Retro-style superstar

In early May 1993, BMW staged an elaborate send-off in the South of France for retiring chairman of the board Eberhard von Kuenheim. After being appointed to the post by principal shareholder Herbert Quandt in 1970, von Kuenheim spent the next two decades transforming BMW from a small provincial automaker into a global powerhouse. To celebrate his achievements, the company brought a fleet of vintage BMW automobiles to St. Tropez, where von Kuenheim and other executives could experience the panorama of BMW history.

"I happened to be with von Kuenheim when he was driving the 507," Chris Bangle told me in 2021. "That was the trigger for the whole chain of events that led to the Z8."

The 507 made a strong impression on all of the board members who drove it, Bangle said, prompting them to wonder why BMW made nothing like it at the time.

In fact, BMW had been working on a large roadster project for several years. After two 8 Series variants were rejected as too heavy, BMW began developing a large roadster based on the E39 5 Series. Identified internally as the

E51, the car was set to be equipped with the folding hardtop deemed essential to compete in the luxury class. A folding hardtop presented serious challenges to both engineering and design, however, as the mechanisms were bulky and placed weight up high on the chassis, exactly where BMW's engineers didn't want it.

"We spent all of our time trying to get around those issues, and not on what a modern roadster should look like," Bangle said. "The engineers were going crazy, because the screws were on them to make this retractable hardtop work. We were just trying to get the package down so that the engineering guys, design guys, and aerodynamic guys were all on the same page, but the designs that came out were all very hefty, with big shoulders."

The E51 was meant to be a modern car, employing BMW's contemporary design language of the early 1990s. The models displayed varying degrees of luxury and sportiness, and all but one (by Thomas Sycha, now head of MINI design) had provision for a folding hardtop. "None were trying to be retro, because there was this fear of God of retro at the time," Bangle said.

Alongside those cars, the design department had built another clay model dubbed the E507 but identified internally as "Truck." This car eschewed BMW's then-current design language for a retro-styled aesthetic inspired by the 507. The E507 was a sort of "skunkworks" project, done absent the E51's packaging requirements for the folding hardtop and other practical details, and with no need to compete against Mercedes.

"[Dr. Wolfgang] Reitzle was the one who, from his rational side, launched everyone down the E51 path to try to solve the problem of the retractable hardtop," Bangle said, "but then his emotional side told us to do one that's a 507, pure. I think we had five or six E51s in the lineup, and this car, which obviously couldn't take a retractable hardtop. And everybody said, 'That's it.'"

The E507's exterior had been sketched (below) by Danish-born Henrik Fisker, who'd joined BMW in 1989 following his graduation from Art Center College of Design in Vevey, Switzerland. Assigned first to BMW Technik, he designed the E1 concept shown at Frankfurt in 1991. Where the E1 was a tidy, battery-powered city car, Fisker's roadster was a soul-stirring sports car that paid direct homage to the 507

in its horizontal kidneys, sculpted fenders, and chromed air outlets, as well as its elegant yet energetic proportions.

Equally evocative was the E507's interior, conceptualized by Scott Lempert—an American Art Center grad who joined BMW in 1991—in collaboration with studio leader Michael Ninic.

In the summer of 1994, the top-ranked E51 proposals for exterior (by Gerd Friedrichs) and interior (by David Carp, a BMW designer since 1992, following his graduation from Art Center) were presented to the board of management alongside the E507. Like Reitzle, the other board members agreed that the E507 offered the most passionate solution to BMW's large roadster problem. The E51 project was abandoned, and soon thereafter the E507 was moving forward under the development code E52.

The car was proceeding as presented, with Fisker's exterior and the interior by Lempert and Ninic. (Fisker had advocated for Carp's sporty-yet-minimalist interior, but the board deemed the Lempert/Ninic concept a better fit for the E52.) The design was "locked in" by the summer of 1994, and most of the basic design work for the dashboard, center console and doors had been completed by the time Lempert left BMW

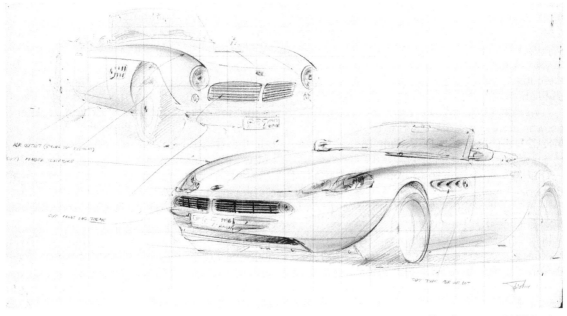

Sketch courtesy BMW Design

in 1995 for a job with Volkswagen in Spain. In his absence, Ninic worked through the remaining details and production requirements for the interior through 1996 and into '97, with assistance from Bruno Amatino in the later stages.

On the exterior side, Fisker did the same prior to his 1997 departure for DesignworksUSA. "I became intensely passionate about this project as it felt like I was designing using the ultimate BMW DNA as my starting point," Fisker told Petrolicious. "It was such a pure project. I only had five engineers working with me, and we had absolutely no restraints. That's why the design could be so pure, because it didn't go through the traditional channels."

Indeed, those engineers came not from the series-production side, but from Dr. Göschel's Special Vehicles division. Like Fisker, Göschel was intrigued by the idea of building a 507-inspired roadster, but he wasn't content to build something retro. "The 507 is a nice-looking car, but the technology is frugal," Göschel told me.

Göschel's vision for the new roadster was anything but frugal. Though its folding hardtop had been jettisoned in favor of a conventional soft top, the renamed E52 was conceived as a no-expense-spared supercar, one that would be as innovative as the Z1 under its retro-styled skin. The Special Vehicles engineers eschewed BMW's usual steel unit body for an aluminum space frame, which kept weight low without compromising safety. Like the 507, the E52 would have aluminum bodywork and a V8 engine, here located behind the front axle as on the Z1. Rather than the series-production M60 V8 the board had requested, Göschel insisted upon the S62 V8—a new engine developed at Motorsport for the as-yet unreleased E39 M5, which delivered an additional 100 horsepower over the M60. "Not all of the old guys were satisfied, but it was the right decision!" Göschel said.

Z07: Tokyo show preview

By 1997, BMW was ready to show the E52 to the public, though not in its final production form. Instead, BMW would display a concept called the Z07—a portmanteau of "Z" and "507." With Fisker in California, the task of building the show car's exterior was assigned to Adrian van Hooydonk, while Carp would create its interior. **(Both are seen in the 2009 photo below, with van Hooydonk in the driver's seat and Carp leaning over to look at the door panels.)** The two started sketching in May 1997,

Z07 interior photo by Helmut Werb

and the car needed to be finished in time for the Tokyo motor show that October. With no capacity to build it at BMW in Munich, Carp and van Hooydonk spent the summer at a prototype and model-building shop in Paris.

To make the project even more challenging, the car needed to be shown not only as a roadster, but as a coupe—like that sketched by Fisker in 1995, then rendered in clay with a Zagato-style double-bubble roof. Since they couldn't show two cars in Tokyo, van Hooydonk and Carp contrived a removable hardtop, which a pair of BMW Design employees would remove and replace every half-hour, allowing journalists to see the car in both coupe and roadster configurations.

"Adrian had to come up with a seamless transition from the roadster to the coupe, which he did in alignment with Henrik, who'd already designed the coupe by 1995," Carp told me in 2021. "By early 1996, there had been a request to see if it could be realized with a common deck lid between the roadster and the coupe, which would save a lot of money. Obviously, it was possible to have a more flowing [coupe] roofline without a carryover roadster decklid, so that is the version which was put on the show car."

Van Hooydonk gave the roadster's decklid an "aerofin" behind the driver's seat that recalled the one on the Jaguar D-type of the 1950s. "That was done simply because it emphasized the roadster even more," Carp said, "and because it looked cool…a very good reason!"

Inside, special touches abound

If van Hooydonk's challenge was formidable, Carp's was no less so. "The interior of the Z07 needed a lot of original design work, because I was only given the surfaces and basic details from the instrument panel, console, and door panels," Carp said. "In order to help Adrian realize the racing roadster image better, I designed the seats so that the top of the passenger seat back would be below the beltline if the headrest were removed. This made it possible for us to put a passenger-side tonneau cover over that half of the car—if you look carefully at photos of the open roadster,

you can see all the little Tenax fastener pins lining the passenger half of the car!"

The interior's crowning feature was its steering wheel—a slender rim that connected to the center section via four sets of wire spokes.

"The idea for a steering wheel with four wire spokes came from Chris Bangle," Carp said. "There was already a traditional three-spoke design underway for the production Z8, but Chris wanted something more 'purist' and sports car-like. He specifically asked me to do a wheel that would have a spoke at 12 o'clock in the straight-ahead position. With the instrument binnacle out of the way, it would finally be possible to see a cool steering wheel through the windshield. It had already been decided that, as a car for sports car purists, there should be no buttons messing up the steering wheel. I was happy to oblige, and the only modern elements were the theoretically plausible space for an airbag, and the thumb grips at 9 and 3 o'clock. Those I designed not only for comfort, but also so their curve would echo the curve found where the dashboard's painted surface continued into the door."

As a complementary touch, van Hooydonk created a retro-style filler cap for the rear decklid that provided a visual link to Carp's steering wheel. Neither of those elements was expected to see production, nor was a production future guaranteed for the car itself—at least not officially—even as the Z07 became the star of the Tokyo motor show.

BMW's press release began with a question, "Z07: Dream, or Possibility?" After stating that "a decision has not yet been made as to whether the ready-to-drive study, which has been worked out down to the last detail, should be further developed for series production," the release went on to describe the car's design highlights and technical details, along with its lineage in the 507.

"The genetic makeup of the Z07 is unmistakable. Behind an elongated front is a low, very flat windshield. The smoothly flowing lines of the wheel arches are absorbed by the wide door and introduced into the powerful haunches. This line gives the Z07 its

elegant, smooth side view. The gills between the front radius section and the door, as well as the large wheels, complete the image of a BMW sports car.

"If you look at the Z07 from the front, you will recognize a familiar face: small round headlights behind glass, and a pronounced double-kidney grille are among the traditional stylistic elements of every BMW. The rear derives its character from the interaction of the wide wheel arches and the slightly sloping line of the rear cover, with a distinctive aerofin behind the driver's seat and the diffuser on the lower rear end, which is framed by two tailpipes made of polished steel.

"No question about it, the Z07 is pure fascination and emotion."

Regardless of the question posed by the press release, Georg Kacher assured the readers of *Automobile* magazine that the car would indeed be built. Its name would be Z8, and it would be available as a roadster and a coupe, with roadster volumes projected at 1,500 and coupe volumes at 3,500 cars. Tooling limitations would keep total volume to around 5,000 cars, making the Z8 an exclusive proposition even before its price—more than $100,000, making it the first BMW to push past that "glass barrier"—and exotic specifications were taken into account.

From show car to production

Not long after the Z07's triumphant debut at Tokyo, BMW finalized its production plans for the Z8. The coupe was canceled, and the car would continue as a roadster only. Even so, the design team would face an uphill battle to get it into production without compromising its stylistic integrity.

As Bangle explained, "You go into all these loop phases, and if you're a more conceptual designer you want to get on to the next project. It's difficult to get dragged through meeting after meeting, but you have to nail down all these little details. On the Z8, they were legion."

With Fisker in California, future Rolls-Royce design chief Ian Cameron and longtime BMW designer Boyke Boyer (responsible for the E30 and E36 3 Series, as well as the E38 7 Series)

were charged with getting the Z8's exterior across the line. Newly appointed interior design chief Michael Ninic, meanwhile, ensured that the Z8's interior would be truly special—and distinctly analog. (Ninic would continue to lead BMW's interior design team until 2008, when he died unexpectedly at just 53.)

"The purity of the cockpit experience was extremely important," Carp told me. "Chris said that the Z8 driver wouldn't be getting into a rental car, where you could expect to find everything you need fairly quickly, but into a car which only the owner/driver need understand. He wanted the owner/driver to have an intimate experience with the car, which no superfluous functions would mask, and where a little experience would show where all the necessary functions were. It was his wish that we not label or illuminate any of the switches— we expected the driver to operate them all with a little practice. This was not a touch-screen experience, but a tactile one."

Indeed, everything the driver or passenger would touch with two fingers had to be authentic—real aluminum for the HVAC knobs, for instance, not metalized plastic.

From the Z07 concept, Carp's wire-spoked steering wheel was championed by Dr. Reitzle as "the only steering wheel that was right for the car." The wheel got a working airbag in the center, and the spokes at 12 o'clock were removed in a concession to Australian regulations that required a speedometer directly in front of the driver. Had the Z8 been sold from new in Australia, Carp says a MINI-style speedo would have been attached to the steering column. In the production Z8, as on the Z07, the instruments are off to the side, directly below the rear-view mirror.

"That's what makes driving the Z8 like riding a motorcycle," Bangle told me. "The viewing triangle—between looking straight ahead, to the rear-view mirror, and to the speedometer— is much smaller than when the instruments are down below, and you've got to track way up to the mirror and back. There's nothing in front to distract you."

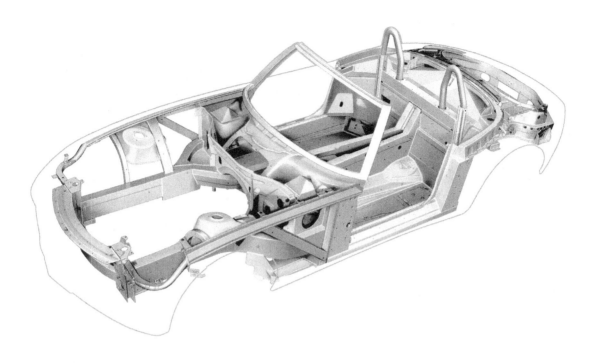

The Z8's bodywork would be rendered in aluminum, attached to BMW's first aluminum space frame. It was built at BMW's Dingolfing plant, where the aluminum beams were extruded and welded to pressed panels. No castings were used, as their fracture behavior at junction points was deemed insufficient. Though it added a touch of exoticism, the aluminum frame was actually cheaper to build than a conventional steel shell at the Z8's low production volume. (Along with the Z8, the Rolls-Royce Phantom rides on an aluminum space frame, which was developed and built with exceptional speed thanks to the know-how gained from the Z8 project.)

The frame's Y-shaped construction offered exceptional safety. The tunnel support provided a strong connection between the front of the car and the rear, while diagonal connection units extended from the side sills to the longitudinal arms to lower the sills and provide a tighter connection between the passenger compartment and the rest of the car. The front clip was bolted rather than welded on, and the frame could be repaired at an ordinary BMW dealer. The body panels bolted to the chassis, allowing for easy replacement should they become damaged.

The space frame weighed just over 500 pounds, and it proved exceptionally stiff. In static measurement, 10,500 Newton-meters of force were required to bend it one degree, while its dynamic stiffness registered at 21 Hertz.

Borrowing from the M5

The Z8's suspension components were executed in aluminum, as well, minimizing unsprung weight to optimize handling. The front suspension is a modified version of the MacPherson strut arrangement used on the E39 5 Series and E38 7 Series, which BMW described as "a double-joint spring strut axle with rack and pinion steering, an aluminum track control arm, tie rod, and anti-roll bar." The Z8 got its own spring and damper rates, with the springs angled to the struts to minimize friction. At the rear, the Z8 used the multi-link rear suspension introduced on the Z1, with an anti-roll bar and extra-large rubber bushings to isolate vibration.

At Göschel's insistence, the Z8 shared its drivetrain with the E39 M5, but the 4,941cc S62 V8 received a few modifications specific to the Z8 where intake and exhaust air flow were concerned. The Z8 got a symmetrical airbox that drew air through two intake air silencers, and two hot-film air mass meters in the air collector. Underhood space was limited, but the engineers were able to avoid any small-diameter intake passageways that would have restricted power. The exhaust system was adapted from the E39 M5, here tuned to deliver a deeper rumble while eliminating high-frequency noises. The idea was to communicate the Z8's purpose to those inside and outside the cabin while still complying with sound regulations worldwide.

Otherwise, the S62 featured individual throttle bodies for each cylinder, four valves per cylinder, and Double VANOS variable valve timing on the intake and exhaust cams. Engine management was via BMW's MS S52 system, which used drive-by-wire operation and allowed more sensitive throttle operation at the flick of the Sport button. A six-speed Getrag Type D manual was the only transmission available, and a limited-slip differential allocated the S62's 394 (SAE, US-spec) horsepower at 6,600 rpm and 368 pound-feet at 3,800 rpm to the rear wheels.

Interestingly, the Z8 tipped the scales at 3,494 pounds to the M5's 4,024 pounds, yet its zero-to-60 mph acceleration was a claimed 4.7 seconds to the M5's 4.8 seconds. The M5 had a sizable aerodynamic advantage, with a Cd of 0.31 to the Z8's 0.43, but one suspects that BMW was quoting a conservative figure for the Z8. As tested by *Road & Track*, the Z8 ran the zero-to-60 mph dash in 4.5 seconds, while the M5 reached 60 mph in BMW's claimed 4.8 seconds.

The Z8's brakes were sourced from the 750i, with 13.15-inch rotors and two-piston calipers up front, 12.9-inch rotors with single-piston calipers at the rear. ABS was standard, as was Cornering Brake Control and Dynamic Stability Control III. The latter was calibrated exclusively for the Z8, with a higher threshold of intervention than in BMW's sedans—on the Nürburgring, the Z8's lap time with DSC III engaged was only a few seconds slower than the 8 minutes, 15 seconds

needed to lap the Nordschleife with DSC off.

The Z07's center-lock magnesium wheels didn't make the transition from concept to production, but the Z8's 18-inch wheels used a similar five-spoke design in aluminum with conventional five-bolt hubs. The wheels were shod with run-flat tires, marking BMW's first use of this technology.

Elsewhere, the Z8 got BMW's first Xenon headlights, and the world's first neon turn signals and brake lights. The brake lights were said to illuminate ten times faster than conventional incandescent lighting, reducing the likelihood of a rear-end collision should the Z8 stop abruptly. Other "firsts" included an electronic steering lock, a separate starter button, and a multifunction radio with GPS and a mobile phone.

The first show, press, and development cars were built in late 1998 and throughout 1999, and the Z8 was shown at Frankfurt in September 1999.

Two months later, the Z8 appeared in the James Bond film, *The World Is Not Enough*. BMW supplied three prototypes, which were kept covered and well guarded when they weren't part of the action, away from potential leaks to the press. (The Z8's role in the film wasn't announced until July 1999.) The car appears in scenes set in the oil fields around Baku, Azerbaijan, menaced by a sawblade-equipped helicopter that finally slices it in half. Fortunately, the car sawn in half was a replica, not the real thing.

Shortly thereafter, the car was introduced to the automotive press in Pasadena, California. Following a long day's drive along coastal and mountain roads, the press raved about the Z8's design, technological innovations, and performance. The car fared well in later comparison tests, too, coming up just short of matching the Ferrari 360 Spyder when *Car and Driver* tested both cars (and an Aston Martin DB7 Vantage Volante) at Monza, Italy and on nearby country roads. Praising the Z8's powertrain, *Car and Driver* declared that "the chassis is rigid enough to harness this thrust without any creaks or groans. The suspension also makes good use of its wide and grippy 18-inch Dunlop SP Sport 9000A tires. But despite this firm grasp on the tarmac, most of us felt slightly timid about pushing the Z8 to its limits."

Testers noted that the Z8 was easy to drive quickly at first, but didn't inspire the confidence of the Ferrari when pushed. A windy cockpit was also judged problematic: "These top-down shenanigans are directly related to the Z8's vintage, upright stance. 'You seem to sit on this car, rather than in it.' Several of us who liked the Z8's vintage fashion statement 'loved the interior treatment and finish' and found the steering wheel to be 'a work of art.'"

Enduring value

While the press was dissecting its flaws, the public was snapping up Z8s as fast as BMW could build them, often paying a premium above the car's $128,570 base price. The Z8 was the most expensive BMW to date, but it was well worth the money to those who got one of 5,703 built. (3,160 were sold new in Europe, while 2,543 were sold in the US.)

"Near the end of the production cycle," Bangle said, "I argued fervently that the last ten examples should be kept aside and 'given' to the remaining living greats of car design—like [Giorgetto] Giugiaro, [Marcelo] Gandini, Chuck Jordan, [Ercole] Spada, [Leonardo] Fioravanti, and a bunch of others—for each to make their own 'Interpretation 507' designs, keeping only the chassis, running gear, and windscreen and seat frames the same. We would execute their designs, make all the examples in aluminum, and have the world's most valuable collection of works by those greats. It didn't fly."

Would that it had! Even so, the production Z8s have proven remarkably durable where both construction and value are concerned. Today, even well-used examples command in excess of $100,000, with low-mileage cars trading for more than twice that when they become available. More important, their performance remains exhilarating even by current standards, and their appearance is every bit as alluring as it was two decades earlier.

Alpina V8 Roadster: Something different

Having begun as a vendor of Weber carburetor kits for the *Neue Klasse* sedan in 1965, Alpina moved on to full BMW tuning packages before being granted manufacturer status by the German Transport Authority in 1983. Subsequent Alpinas were still based on BMWs, but with nicer interiors, more refined suspension, stronger brakes, and more powerful engines. They also included technological innovations like forced induction, state-of-the-art engine management, catalytic converters, bulletproof cooling systems, and optional automatic transmissions that didn't sap engine performance while allowing manual gear selection from buttons on the steering wheel.

Introduced in 1992 and evolved continuously since, Alpina's Switch-Tronic automatic was the crucial piece of technology behind the transformation of the Z8 into the Alpina V8 Roadster. The project was led by Andy Bovensiepen, son of Alpina founder Burkhard Bovensiepen, then working at BMW rather than the family firm. Bovensiepen's efforts brought classic Alpina refinement to the lovely E52 platform.

Where the Z8 was available only with a manual transmission, the Alpina V8 Roadster was available only with the five-speed Switch-Tronic.

The transmission smoothed out the Z8's rougher edges, highlighting its Grand Touring character. So did Alpina's use of its own 4,837cc V8 in place of the Z8's Motorsport-developed S62.

Where the US-spec S62 put out 394 horsepower at 6,600 rpm, the Alpina V8 delivered 381 horsepower at 5,800 rpm. Where the S62 put out 368 pound-feet at 3,800 rpm, the Alpina V8 yielded 384 pound-feet at the same engine speed. It was a better match for the automatic transmission, but it also made the V8 Roadster slightly slower than the Z8 from zero to 60 mph: 5.0 seconds rather than 4.7 (claimed). It compensated with a higher top speed, 161 rather than 155 mph, but it contributed to the Alpina's reputation as a *boulevardier*.

So did the Alpina's softer suspension, which was tuned to accommodate the car's 20-inch wheels and low-profile tires, as well as a 15mm lower ride height. Plenty of enthusiasts preferred the Alpina suspension, and the V8 Roadster's conventional rather than run-flat tires.

In 2003, Alpina built 555 examples of the V8 Roadster, 450 of which were sold through BMW dealers in the US for $137,595. It was Alpina's first official offering in this country, but it wouldn't be the last. Although the firm kept its smaller cars in Europe, several generations of B7s have been offered in the US, along with the current XB7 SAV and B8 coupe.

Photos by Helmut Werb

Z8 Coupe: Inspired, but unbuilt

Although a coupe version of the E52 had been drawn by Henrik Fisker in 1995 and rendered in clay by 1996, the Z07 concept would be built only as a roadster prior to its debut at the Tokyo motor show in 1997. With no budget to show both body styles, Adrian van Hooydonk and David Carp built the Z07 with a removable hardtop that simulated a full-on coupe. At the Tokyo show, it would be removed and replaced every half-hour.

Writing about the Z07 for *Automobile* magazine's January 1998 issue, Georg Kacher noted that BMW planned to build 1,500 roadsters and 3,500 coupes. In truth, the BMW board had already rejected the coupe for production, and the Z8 was built only as a roadster.

The hardtop that was delivered with each new Z8 was meant to suffice in lieu of a fixed-roof coupe, but the desire for a genuine Z8 coupe refused to die. In 2002, designer Ian Cameron worked with the Special Vehicles team to build a pair of Z8 coupe prototypes. Atop standard Z8 bodywork, the coupes were equipped with a fixed roof that featured the Zagato-style double-bubble roof included in Fisker's concept sketch, plus the striking buttresses borrowed from the Z07 concept's hardtop. The latter recalled the buttresses on certain coachbuilt Ferraris by Pininfarina of the 1950s, albeit in less exaggerated form.

Unfortunately, the board again decided not to build this Z8-based coupe, and to let the model expire in 2003. "It came down to the wire, and it was really tragic that Ian couldn't get it through [to production]," said Chris Bangle in 2021.

"The coupe had the Zagato roof and much less weight," said Dr. Göschel told me, clearly still excited by the model, "but the board refused to build it." (Göschel himself was on the board by then, having become head of R&D in March 2000.)

One Z8 coupe prototype was reportedly destroyed in a testing crash, but the other was preserved at BMW Classic in Munich, where it was photographed by Helmut Werb in 2019. The Zagato-style roof would live on, as well, crowning the Z4 coupe of 2006-'08. It was also used, most appropriately, on the BMW Zagato Coupe concept built in collaboration with that illustrious Italian *carrozzeria* in 2012.

Sketch courtesy BMW Design

GINA
The paradigm shift

Before we move on to the next roadster in BMW's succession of Z cars, let's depart from the strict chronology to explore what was happening behind the scenes at BMW just before the dawn of the 20th century.

After 100 years of relatively linear evolution, the automotive industry was faced with an unprecedented—and somewhat contradictory—set of challenges. Customers were demanding ever-greater performance and sophistication, while governments were demanding that cars meet increasingly stringent regulations for occupant and pedestrian safety. All of those demands made cars larger and heavier—just as governments were calling for drastic reductions in fuel consumption and emissions, both of which were easier to achieve with smaller, lighter vehicles.

From the engineering side, BMW solved part of the problem with new engine technologies like Valvetronic butterfly-less throttle operation and the widespread use of turbocharging, all of which would fall under the EfficientDynamics banner a few years later. Weight was reduced through the greater use of aluminum, magnesium, and even carbon fiber, with M cars

the prime beneficiaries of the latter material.

Addressing the size of the cars—or, more accurately, keeping them attractive and effective as they grew— required an intervention from the design side, one that would blend aesthetics and technology in unprecedented ways.

"Not all designers believe in the forward movement of their craft, but I do, and BMW Design did at that time," Chris Bangle told me in 2021. "By this, I refer to the process of change: transformation, evolution, perhaps even revolution of the state of the art into something new, fresh, inspiring, and appealing in new ways, which can engage audiences in a new manner and solve new problems."

A graduate of Art Center College of Design in Pasadena, Bangle started his career at Opel in 1981 before moving to Fiat in 1985. In 1992, he was named head of BMW Design following a two-year interregnum that followed the unexpected resignation of his predecessor, Claus Luthe, in 1990.

As the '90s wore on, Bangle and his team were faced with cars that were getting bigger and heavier, as were their human drivers. "Design must do many things, and like fashion, it must

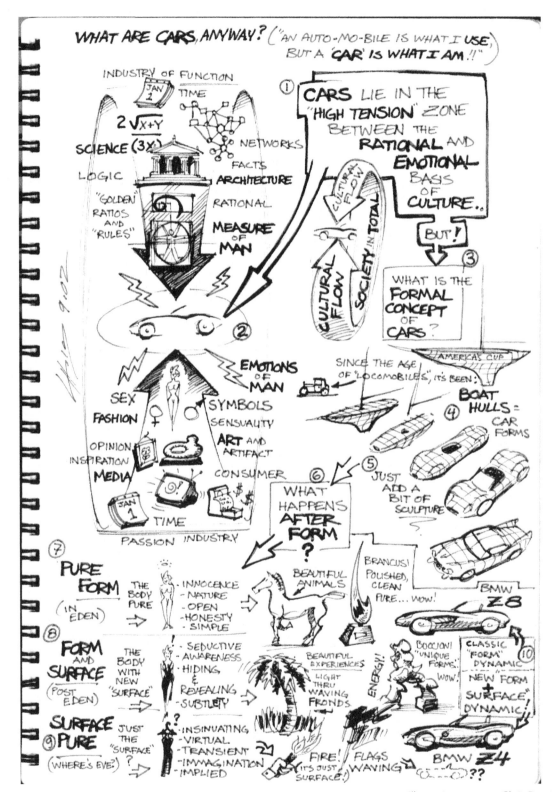

Illustration courtesy Chris Bangle

convince you that the girl or guy underneath is still sexy, despite putting on the pounds."

As an example, Bangle cited the design process behind the E65 7 Series, which began in 1998. "With the transition from E38 to E65, we had to absorb a hood 60mm (2.4 inches) higher for those super-efficient engines. You have to push [the driver] up to see over it, and people were taller to begin with, I think by about 8mm. They need additional headroom but, Ooops! Forgot! More airbags overhead! We also needed more rear legroom, and 57-way power rear seats that add thickness, so that means the rear head arc is going back even further. We need better aero, too, but the wheels are the same size and the overall length is the same! With the roof so high and pushed back and no increase in rear overhang, doing a radical trick with the ass-end was the only option."

The E65 offered one solution, but Bangle knew that addressing the problem successfully meant re-thinking not just the clothing, but the car underneath it. BMW's design and manufacturing processes needed to change dramatically, but getting the budget for the necessary experiments wouldn't be easy.

"One of my standard ploys was to take the previous production car's design and mill it directly on the new package, stretched and enlarged to match," Bangle said. "Those monstrosities quickly put to bed the Reitzlian dictum, 'We know our design' that had driven the incremental changes at BMW up until then."

Reaching for the pole

To Bangle, repeating what had already been done was insufficient. "We believed our designs should not be 'what our forefathers chose not to do,' but 'what could not be thought of before we did it.' When car design was really doing its job right, it could be summed up in one word: endeavor. That came from Werner Haumeyr, then running the GINA build and now head of modeling. He said, 'You don't reach for the South Pole by going a few steps farther than the last guy and calling it a success. You go for all of it, the whole distance, or die in the attempt.'"

The metaphorical South Pole involved not just aesthetics, but one of the design department's perpetual challenges: how to translate sketches into sheet metal.

Series-production car bodies are welded and glued together from large sheets of steel stamped in giant presses, a hugely expensive process. "Every design director was struggling with the question of how many stamp-passes the designs in their sheet metal would require," Bangle said. "Having to tone down the depth and detail in the sheet metal to appease the gods of stamping was one of the key drivers making all cars look the same."

To break free from established practices and results, Bangle turned to DesignworksUSA, BMW's newly-acquired subsidiary in Newbury Park, California. The firm had been founded in 1972 by Chuck Pelly, one of Bangle's instructors at Art Center. Pelly had designed the driver and passenger seats for the E31 8 Series before selling a partial stake in DesignworksUSA to BMW in 1991. Four years later, he sold the entire company to BMW.

Even after becoming a wholly-owned BMW subsidiary, DesignworksUSA continued to work for outside clients. Before the start of his research project, Bangle had asked designers working on non-car projects to offer their suggestions for what a car could be. Among the half-dozen ideas presented was one from Fernando Pardo (in photo on page 83, top), a young Venezuelan who'd joined Designworks following his 1986 graduation from the University of Cincinnati. The exterior of Pardo's model consisted of a nylon stocking stretched over a framework, which he named "Gina" after the stripper who'd inspired it.

The concept wasn't entirely new, as fabric-covered frameworks had been used on everything from covered wagons to airplanes and dirigibles, but it had never been used in this specific way. "Textile cars were always about function—bigger, smaller, that sort of thing," Bangle said. "Fernando should get credit for discovering that there is emotion in a textile car. No one had thought of that before."

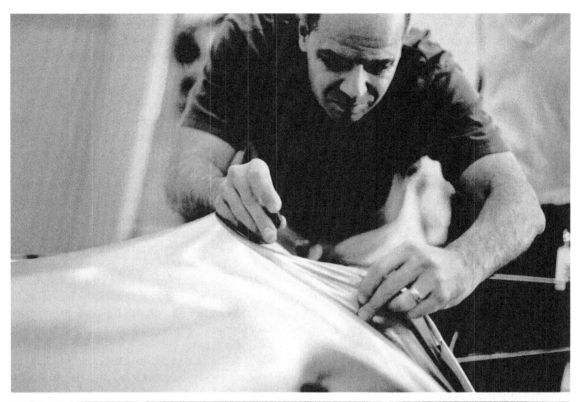

After seeing Pardo's model at Designworks, Bangle stopped in New York on his way back to Munich. Visiting an exhibit on Textiles in Architecture at Materials Connexion, he had an epiphany: that a fabric exterior could eliminate the investment cost in tooling required to stamp bodywork in steel.

Getting the budget to build it

That proved key to unlocking the budget, and Bangle went straight from the Munich airport to a weekend retreat for BMW executives. "I buttonholed all of them, babbling about zero investment and the customer's ability to update their exteriors every year. They thought I was nuts, I'm sure, but I got immediate support from Clemens Schmitz-Justen, then running the body-in-white group; he and Gero Kamp in Manufacturing Innovation got me in with the tooling guys. They were only half-convinced that we could out-design them, telling me, 'Anything you can do in textile, we can do in metal.'"

Bangle appealed to those in charge of BMW's research budget, arguing that incredible savings could be achieved by eliminating tooling, and emphasizing fabric's ecological benefits: "It's ten times better than painted steel, but only one-third better than unpainted steel, which shows how un-ecological the painting process is." The project had benefits for research into rapid manufacturing, as well, where textiles seemed like "the perfect mate to under-the-skin innovations."

The project became known as GINA, the stripper's name having given way to a more family-friendly acronym: "Geometry and Functions In 'N' Adaptions." According to Bangle, the N refers to "an unquantified sum applied to a large but finite set of circumstances."

In the rush to realize the ideas it contained, the project's scope was reined in somewhat. "The car is actually called GINA Light, not because of its weight, but because we only got in a fraction of the innovation we had planned for it," Bangle said.

Ah, but what innovation there was!

Evocative forms

Having secured the budget to build a full-scale prototype, Bangle asked DesignworksUSA's designers to define the aesthetic. At this stage, Pardo's model lost out to a concept presented by Anders Warming (at far right in the photo opposite, bottom). Warming's concept expressed the design language set to appear on the forthcoming Z4, which he'd designed a year earlier. GINA would serve as a preview for that radically redesigned roadster, though its true purpose went beyond aesthetics.

"This whole idea of understanding surface as a thing in and of itself, instead of surface as just being the outside of a volume..." Bangle told me in 2021. "That was the critical switch that the Z4 showcased, but which had already started when we were dealing with GINA, which had no volume, just surface. GINA really changed our thinking about where surfaces could go."

In Munich, design engineer Mario Greco constructed an aluminum framework atop a Z8 rolling chassis. This would be covered by an exceptionally durable, heat-resistant, water-repellent, and highly flexible fabric that would give the car a unified form created by tension and pressure, either positive or negative. ("Greco went on to invent a lightweight folded metal forming process at Industrial Origami and later ALCOA," Bangle said.)

Just as interesting, the framework was movable, allowing the car to change shape upon command. In an evocative move, it could reveal its engine through a slit atop its hood. (Ostensibly, this was done to permit access to the oil filler cap.) No less suggestively, GINA could raise its rear spoiler or extend its rocker panels, adding aerodynamic stability while changing the car's mood.

Because the volume of fabric remained constant, it stretched during some functions and folded during others. Opening the doors, for instance, created a rouched cascade at the hinges. The headlights, taillights, and turn signals, meanwhile, were hidden beneath the fabric, invisible until illuminated.

GINA was no less innovative in the cockpit, and no less adaptable. Sleek and uncluttered,

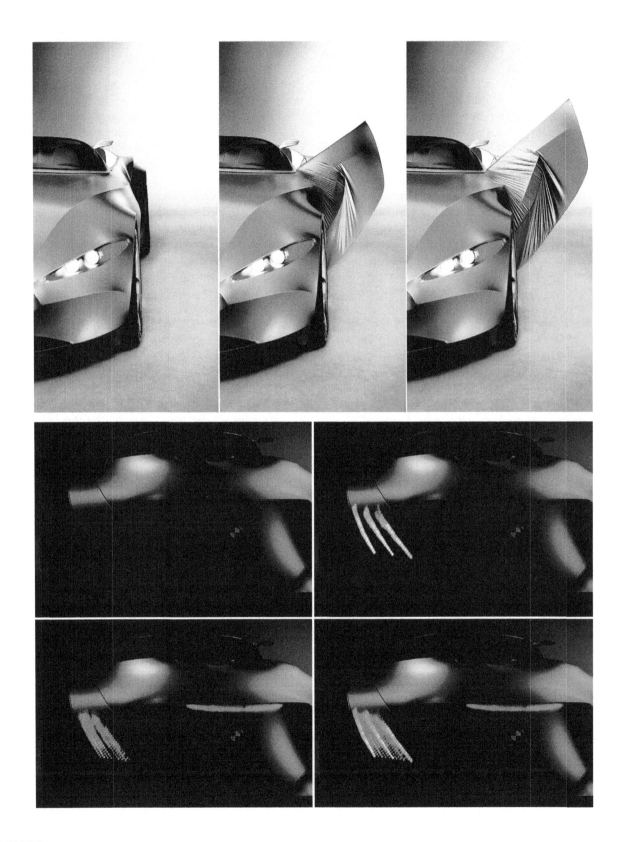

it could change its shape to fit the bodies of its occupants. Behind the fabric covered dashboard, gauges and other indicators appeared only when illuminated, and only when the driver demanded them.

Outside forces

Bangle had hoped to present GINA at a TED conference in October 2001, but that plan was canceled when the automotive press—and a vocal segment of BMW's traditional customer base—failed to embrace the company's new styling direction.

First, the radical X coupé had been met with derision at the Detroit auto show in January 2001. That summer, the E65 7 Series was previewed in Munich, and the press responded with more skepticism. The E65's formal debut at Frankfurt 2001 coincided with the terror attacks of September 11, which cast a pall worldwide.

If all of that weren't enough, BMW had recently severed its ill-fated connection with the Rover group, absorbing huge losses just as the company was making a costly re-entry into Formula One. The purse strings were tightened across the board, and a lot of innovative projects were canceled.

With BMW Design on the hot seat, GINA was parked in the basement of the FIZ. It might have languished there forever had Bangle not commissioned a video that presented GINA in all "her" sensual glory a few years later. The cat was out of the bag, and BMW had no choice but to allow the car to make its debut.

In 2008, GINA went on display at the BMW Museum in Munich. By then, the public had assimilated the "flame surfaced" aesthetic via the Z4, and BMW Design had incorporated much of what had been learned with GINA on other cars, including the aforementioned 5 Series. "For everyone at design who was involved with GINA, it had huge ripple effects through our thinking," Bangle said.

One of its most important effects was freeing designers to utilize "negative surface," such as that used by David Arcangeli to mask the volume of the E60 5 Series. "Before that, all surfaces were positive (convex), and if there was a negative or concave surface to be seen, it was always a radius between planes. Negative surfaces were de facto banned after the Citroen Dyane poisoned the well for everyone," Bangle said. "Design was reaching a dead end in the '90s, because the agreed-upon geometric concept of the surface itself was holding back what computer-aided design could offer. No one knew how to go beyond the planal geometry approach."

That set of aesthetics goes back to the ancient Greeks, but that isn't the only form that beauty can take, as any non-Westerner understands implicitly. GINA's aesthetics allowed designers to escape those boundaries, while its structure allowed them to escape the limitations of modeling in clay, wood, or plaster. Those traditional modeling methods involved executing surfaces that were already known, and which had already been defined mathematically.

Working in fabric was an entirely different process, Bangle said. "With elastic textile held at the perimeter, a surface was no longer one in which it first had to be theoretically clear, then executed perfectly. Instead, it became, 'I don't know what will happen until you stretch it over the frame—try putting that there. Holy f*ck, did you see that? Take a picture; it'll disappear when you let it go!' To make a finished textile car as convincing as GINA took a lot of messing about, just to know how to even make the thing."

Practical applications

Once they figured it out, designers could work with an entirely new set of possibilities. "[Prior to GINA], if you wanted, say, a bulge in the middle of a hood, you had to imagine it as a form that was unique in and of itself, embedded in the underlying hood surface and joined together with the same radiuses that had been with us since the Model T," Bangle explained. "No one knew how to rationally deform the underlying surface until a bulge of some sort emerged, but with GINA's cloth you could easily stick a wire form under it and get all kinds of shapes—no need for radiuses.

"It was this concept that led to the digital embossing technique used on the hood of the Z4 M, and if you look at the sharp edge of the Z4's trunk lid you see that it emerges most naturally out of the surrounding metal, disappearing before it gets to the edge. This sort of shape was difficult even to imagine before GINA."

In the interior, too, GINA opened up new possibilities. Its unadorned and adaptable cockpit foretold the interiors of today's BMWs, particularly on the dashboard. A modern BMW dash presents as blank until the car starts up, when its screens illuminate with gauges and other information. The driver can choose what to display or hide, while buttons and knobs have been reduced or eliminated in favor of touchscreen actuation.

Pushing the boundaries can be liberating, even if one pulls back from them in the end.

"The result was less about using cloth for cars of the future, and more about unleashing the minds of car designers to a new meta-level of how surfaces were formed, until they went from a product—a thing that was described and then made—to a by-product of a process, Bangle said. "GINA released car designers from a fixed mindset of what is correct and what is not. It took a while, but today's exteriors from practically all car companies owe a debt to that car for freeing up creativity."

E85 Z4

Flame-surfaced roadster

As BMW's engineers and designers prepared to replace the popular Z3, they faced all the packaging and design challenges highlighted in the previous chapter on GINA. They also needed to take BMW's small roadster upmarket, where it would compete not against the bare-bones Miata but Porsche's sporty mid-engine Boxster and Mercedes' stylish SLK.

According to Dr. Burkhard Göschel, still in charge of Special Vehicles but soon to be elevated to head Whole Vehicle Development, the success of the Porsche and Mercedes roadsters convinced BMW's marketing department to take the company's roadster upscale: "No more entry-level, fun-to-drive roadster, but a more prestigious car."

Although the new roadster would share a platform and many components with the E46 3 Series, the goal was to create a car whose performance and functionality could match that of the flagship Z8, but at one-third the price, and with much wider availability.

Where the Z8's styling was retro, the new roadster's would be thoroughly modern, with a sleek, angular design from Anders Warming at BMW's DesignworksUSA subsidiary. We've already encountered Warming's exterior design for GINA, but that experimental concept was built after his design had been selected for the new roadster. Had all gone to plan, GINA would have served as a preview for Warming's aesthetically-advanced roadster—his first new car for BMW.

"I hadn't been selected to create the scale model for the roadster," Warming told me in 2021. "I was the kid, surrounded by heavy hitters. I just wanted to hold my own."

Indeed, Warming was just 26 years old, fresh from the Transportation Design program at Art Center College of Design in Vevey, Switzerland and Pasadena, California. Arriving at Designworks in 1998, he found himself working alongside a slightly older cadre of fellow Art Center grads: Z8 designer Henrik Fisker, then heading Designworks' automotive styling department; Chris Chapman, who designed Isuzu's gull-winged XU-1 show car before penning the BMW X5 at Designworks; and Marek Djordjevic, then working on the Rolls-Royce Phantom while also sketching Designworks' proposal for the next-generation roadster. (Chapman was drawing its proposed

coupe counterpart.)

While Djordjevic was still a student at Art Center in Pasadena, the Belgrade-born designer had sketched an unusual roadster that helped him get hired at Designworks following his graduation in 1991. Two years later, it was built into a concept known as the Zetta, the European pronunciation of the letter Z.

"We wanted to turn it into a Z8-based modern roadster," Chris Bangle told me, "so we had it built at G Studio in Torino out of resin blocks. It's a hard model, a non-runner, in black. It had wonderfully tight, flat surfaces—as if you took the Z8 that Henrik Fisker did and made its really evil, sharp, edgy cousin. Anders' work owes a bit of its spiritual roots to what Djordjevic had already done, even though Djordjevic's car never got any further."

The Zetta helped clear the path for innovation, and BMW determined from the outset that its next roadster wouldn't have a retro design like the Z3 or Z8.

"From Day One, the word from the board was 'modern,'" Bangle said. "The Z3 was such a big deal that to escape from it, people had to put in orders like 'No more retro!' to force people into a new mental picture rather than just doing the next Z3."

If Djordjevic's Zetta suggested one possibility, Frank Gehry's recently opened Guggenheim Bilbao suggested another, at least to Warming (**opposite, below**). Assigned to draw Sport Package elements for the E46 3 Series and MINI, Warming began sketching a roadster of his own, inspired by the twisting titanium panels of Gehry's museum. "Marek came by, thought it was great and said, 'Let the kid do it! He's got the chops.' He was ramping up his work on the Rolls-Royce Phantom, and he asked Henrik to let me do the roadster instead. It was a very sweet thing, and I'm grateful."

Even as it departed from the Z3's retro design, Warming's proposal retained a connection to its predecessor, and to BMW's heritage.

"We worked around the 'PSD' strategy: proportion, surface, detail," Warming said. "The car has basic BMW proportions, with the wheels out front, the long hood, the set-back greenhouse, and the stubby rear. Surface is an area where we can break away from tradition, take a different road away from the rounded shapes. With the details, we were BMW-specific, with double-round headlights, double-kidney grille, and round taillights that nod to the 1600 and 2002, and to the cars from the 1930s. Those taillights were quite controversial—I think all the other proposals had rectangular taillights.

"It's a bookend solution, with a new form language flanked by proper BMW proportions and details."

In addition to signature BMW design elements, Warming was hyper-attentive to details like cutlines, where one body panel met another. "If you follow the line from the mirror, up the A-pillar, over the windscreen, under the rocker, and across the hood, it's one continuous line," he said. "Another line is formed by the rear trunk as it cuts into the valence panel. Those were very important to me, giving the car a strict graphic organization."

Once the car had been modeled in clay, Warming, Fisker, and Chapman presented it—along with several other Designworks projects—to design chief Chris Bangle at the FIZ. "We didn't like the overhead light, so we turned that off and just had the evaluation lights on the clay model, like movie lighting. It was the first time Chris saw the full-size model, and he started dancing next to the car. 'I love it! It's like a symphony! Trombone! Violin! Flame!' The evaluation lights were reflecting on the body, and the headlights were making their own flames of light. That's where the term 'flame surfacing' came from."

Warming himself had a different description for his design: sexy math. "It's sexy, but it's mathematically correct," he said. I like juxtaposition and dichotomy, and I like the energy of that phrase. It's precise, analytical, and correct, but beautiful."

The beauty comes not only from the form, but from the juxtaposition of the organic and the mechanistic. Even though the automobile is clearly a machine, it greets onlookers with a warm and inviting human face. Warming says he took inspiration from cars like the Lamborghini

Miura, which he describes as resembling "a human being with incredible character—pretty, but not perfect, and not too aggressive." Accordingly, Warming drew the roadster with its headlight "eyes" wide open, and with its front fascia turned slightly upward, forming a sly smile.

In the summer of 1999, the BMW board of management selected Warming's design for production, choosing it over competing proposals from BMW Design in Munich.

"It was dramatic, and it had everything going for it that BMW wanted," Bangle said. "If the Z8 is Eve before she bites the apple—pure animal sensuality, feminine purity—the Z4 is Eve *after* she bit the apple. She's aware of her nudity, so she covers herself. The whole history of feminine attire includes all kinds of ways where the covering makes the body more enticing than having no covering. The idea behind the Z4 was that the way the covering is pulled on the underlying volumes, which haven't changed since the Z8, makes it more sexy, more enticing, and gives it that slightly devious side."

Those qualities, of course, are also present in GINA, to an even greater degree and in more animated form than in the production roadster.

Warming's car represented a clear break from the Z3, and its selection coincided with a new model-numbering scheme at BMW, in which "special occasion" cars like roadsters and coupes would be assigned even numbers while sedans stuck with the traditional sequence of odd numbers: 3, 5, and 7.

Assigned the development code E85, Warming's car proceeded to the prototype stage in Munich, supervised by Erik Goplen. "They took two Z3s, chopped them up, and added more space from the dash to the front axle—100mm and 200mm," Warming said. "From these two mules, we chose the longer one. The front was in Z8 territory, and I think Erik did a great job in fighting for the right proportions. We also got bigger wheels, which made it sit better, and a slightly lower H-point [where the driver's hip is located when seated]. You're much lower than in a Z3."

Inside the cockpit, the new roadster got a complementary interior from Munich native Oliver Sieghart (**opposite, above**). Like Warming, Sieghart joined BMW right after completing his degree, having studied product design at Munich's *Fachhochschule*, or University of Applied Science. The Z4 would be one of his first projects upon arrival.

Like that of the Z8, the Z4's interior was designed with a minimum of buttons, knobs, and other distractions. Where the retro roadster's dash was all soft curves, however, the Z4's got an intriguing mix of torqued surfaces and crisp angles, usually rendered in metalized plastics but here presented in brushed aluminum that emphasized the car's mechanical nature. It tended toward the austere, but it advanced the game considerably for BMW's interior design department.

That said, its simplicity presented a problem where one important feature was concerned. The interior had been designed without a provision for GPS navigation, which dealers in the US and Japan demanded. The solution was to equip the Z4 with a pop-up screen on the dash, just above the air vents, that remained hidden when not in use.

Precise surfaces, precision engineering

Design proceeded in tandem with engineering, where a similar level of precision was applied to the Z4's chassis and drivetrain. Where the Z3 was built on a strict budget to compete with the inexpensive Miata, the Z4 would compete against the Boxster and SLK, as well as the Audi TT—all far more sophisticated cars.

As David Lightfoot pointed out in his comprehensive *BMW Z4: Design, Development and Production*, BMW began by identifying the Z3's principal weakness: its lack of structural stiffness. "If we wanted a car that is sportier and more precise in handling, steering, and agility, then body stiffness is one of the most important aspects," chief engineer Martin Klanner told Lightfoot.

The engineering team's goal was to match the Z8's performance, but their budget precluded a bespoke aluminum chassis. Instead, the Z4 would start with the E46 3 Series platform, rendered in high-strength steel. As Lightfoot

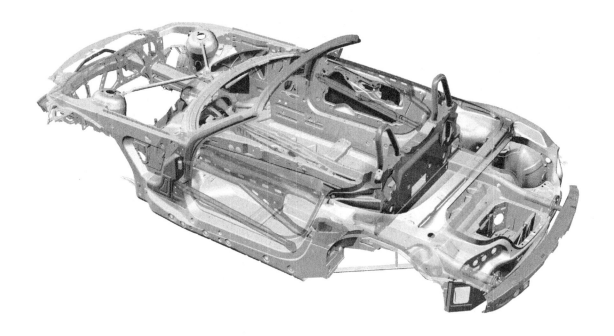

explained, this particular grade of steel wasn't normally available in the US, where the Z4 would be built. Using it required extra effort on the part of BMW's steel supplier, but it proved crucial to achieving the structural stiffness required of the new roadster. Fully assembled, the Z4's torsional stiffness was rated at 14,500 Newton meters for one degree of twist. By contrast, the Z3 needed just 5,600 Newton meters to twist the same amount. The Z4's dynamic stiffness, meanwhile, measured 21 Hertz—not as high as the E46 sedan's 29.8 Hertz, but a significant improvement over the outgoing Z3 M roadster's 18.4 Hertz.

A stiffer chassis makes a car feel more solidly built, and it also allows a car's suspension to work more cleanly throughout its range of motion. Where the suspension was concerned, the Z4 would benefit by using the latest components from the E46 front and rear. The E46's front axle, with its MacPherson strut front suspension, fit easily into the Z4 chassis and worked well straight off the bat. For this application, it got a few weight-saving touches, like forged aluminum lower arms and hollow strut rods.

The E46 rear axle, on the other hand, proved problematic. As Lightfoot explained, BMW's engineers made changes to the shocks, springs, anti-roll bars, and rubber bushings, yet the rear axle still didn't perform as desired in the Z4. Apparently, this had been anticipated from the outset, but the cheaper options needed to be explored before the engineers designed and built a new rear axle carrier and lower control arms, adding a triangular brace to improve rigidity around the axle.

Stiff suspension, aerodynamic stability

The Z4 had a distinctly stiff ride for a BMW, and not only because it inherited the Z8's run-flat tires. Its shock travel was shorter and its spring/damper rates were stiffer than normal, too, because a consistent ride height kept the vehicle's aerodynamic performance more stable. Aerodynamics had become a crucial consideration in light of the Audi TT's much-publicized problems at speed. Soon after its

introduction, the TT was involved in numerous crashes, five of which resulted in fatalities. Audi blamed the crashes on driver error, at least until one killed a former rally driver. That forced Audi to address the TT's design issues, namely its lack of electronic traction control and its rear-axle lift at speed. Traction control was offered as a retrofit, while newly-built TTs got a pop-up rear spoiler.

The TT episode made the other German manufacturers particularly attentive to aerodynamics, and to safety issues in general. BMW had already equipped the Z3 and other automobiles with traction control, and it made sure the Z4 had effective aerodynamics, as well. The E85's front fascia and built-in trunk lid spoiler were designed to create stability-inducing downforce, with more added by the car's underbody. Even so, the car exhibited very low drag for a roadster—Cd 0.35 with the top up—matched with a relatively small frontal area of 1.91 square meters.

Although the Z4's external dimensions weren't much larger than those of the Z3, its footprint increased considerably. The wheelbase expanded from 96.3 inches to 98.2 inches, while wheel tracks increased from 55.6 inches to 58.0 inches front, and from 58.8 inches to 59.7 inches rear. That gave the Z4 a more sure-footed stance, as well as better-balanced handling with reduced understeer.

M54 power, and three transmissions

The Z4 would debut with the familiar M54 six in both 2.5- and 3.0-liter displacements, both tuned for optimum performance in the roadster. (Outside the US, a 170-horsepower 2.2-liter variant was offered, as well.) It was a sports car, after all, so the Z4 got a new intake system that allowed the 3.0-liter engine, in particular, to make more than the quoted 225 horsepower—though how much would remain a mystery without measuring output on the dyno.

New transmission options were also on the agenda. While the 2.5-liter M54 was paired with the familiar Getrag five-speed manual, the 3.0-liter engine got a new six-speed manual built by ZF. A torque-converter Steptronic

automatic from GM was optional, again with five forward gears on the Z4 2.5i, six on the 3.0i. More interestingly, both engines could be mated with a Sequential Manual Gearbox. Derived from Formula One, SMG offered a link to BMW's participation in racing's top-flight series, for which it contributed the engine, gearbox, and electronics used with the Williams F1 chassis starting in 2000.

Further electronics innovation was applied in the form of BMW's sport-oriented Dynamic Traction Control, which replaced Dynamic Stability Control. While it still applied the brakes to keep the car moving in the right direction, this less-intrusive system didn't cut engine power when it detected wheelspin.

The Z4 became the first BMW equipped with Electric Power Steering (EPS) in place of the traditional hydraulic assist. Developed in conjunction with supplier ZF, the EPS system replaced the hydraulic pump with an electronic control unit that processed information from the driver's inputs at the wheel (torque), vehicle speed, and other factors to adjust the level of assist delivered through an electric motor. Because it only provided boost when needed—otherwise remaining "off"—EPS prevented the parasitic power losses of an always-on hydraulic system, and the additional fuel required to counter them. It also had far less internal friction than the hydraulic system. Unfortunately, it also provided less "feel" and feedback through the steering wheel.

To counter that lack of feel, BMW included a power assist variable within the car's Dynamic Drive Control, aka the "Sport" button. When pressed, the Sport button performed its traditional function of making the throttle more direct, and it also reduced power assist to the steering. (Regardless of setting or boost level, the steering ratio remained consistent at 14.2:1—slightly quicker than the late-production Z3's 15.4:1.) In Z4s equipped with SMG, the Sport button allowed the gearbox to shift more quickly, too.

Finally, the Z4 got a soft top that was much improved over that in the Z3. Power-operated, the top was billed as the world's fastest, able to open or close in just ten seconds. More important was the glass rear window in place of the Z3's plastic. Along with greater clarity of vision, it included a built-in defroster.

Moving on up

Like the Z3, the Z4 would be built exclusively by BMW Manufacturing in Spartanburg, South Carolina. Production began in September 2002, just before the Z4's debut at the Paris auto show. Its dramatically different styling aroused mild controversy at Paris, and a derisive response from tradition-minded BMW enthusiasts who'd only seen the car in photos.

Not long after its static debut in Paris, the Z4 was introduced to the world's automotive press in Faro, Portugal. Here, the car's styling received few complaints, its compound curves and sharp edges revealing new complexity in the shifting sunlight.

It drove much better than anyone had expected, too, revealing prodigious mechanical grip on Portugal's twisting seaside roads. "The Z4's ride is firm but not punishing. And in corners, the BMW is absolutely planted. A combination of high grip, good balance and flat weight transfer without body roll give the car a sure-footed, reassuring feel in rapid transitions," reported *Road & Track*. "BMW has made a real change in emphasis with the Z4. It's still a classic roadster—a two-seater with a long hood and the occupants set well back in the car—but it's less a stylish, high-priced alternative to a Miata now, and more a serious, high-performance sports car fit to contend with the likes of the Porsche Boxster, one of its principal rivals."

Bimmer magazine echoed that praise for the car's mechanical grip and overall ride quality, but reserved final judgment until the car could be driven in the US. "We've been fooled before by the better road conditions in Europe, and the pavement we encountered in Portugal was too smooth to compare with what we typically find at home."

As predicted, the Z4 didn't fare as well on America's decaying infrastructure. Especially with Sport Package—which brought even

shorter, stiffer springs and dampers as well as 18-inch wheels and the same run-flat tires—the Z4 was almost undriveable over the bumpy pavement that's normal on just about every fun back road. The rear axle, in particular, simply didn't have enough compliance to cope with irregularities, and trying to put the power down for a rapid corner exit was an exercise in futility.

Electric Power Steering was nettlesome, too. Some drivers barely noticed the change from hydraulics, while others decried the lack of feel and feedback. SMG, on the other hand, was universally reviled. It would be discontinued for the 2006 model year, when the Z4 received a mild cosmetic update consisting of revised bumpers, new rectangular fog lights, and redesigned taillights with adaptive technology that increased illumination according to pedal pressure.

Along with those changes, the updated 2006 Z4 got the new 3.0-liter N52 engine. Featuring a magnesium block and Valvetronic butterfly-less throttle operation, the 2,996cc N52 delivered 214 horsepower and 185 pound-feet in the Z4 3.0i, or 255 horsepower and 220 pound-feet in the sportier Z4 3.0si thanks to a revised intake, exhaust, and electronics.

Throughout its production run, the Z4 won high marks for its spacious interior, high-quality fit and finish, and overall solidity. (It wasn't heavy, though: The Z4 3.0i weighed just 2,998 pounds with a manual transmission.) It was deemed a worthy rival to the Porsche Boxster, as well as a car well worth its $40,995 asking price.

Even so, it failed to capture the imagination of enthusiasts like the Z3 had, and it was hampered further by the difficult economic climate into which it was born. The roadster craze was ebbing, as well: While BMW had sold nearly 300,000 examples of its predecessor, Z4 production was only two-thirds that. Not including the Z4 M Roadster covered below, Z4 production totaled just 175,469 roadsters by the time the last Z4 was built in August 2008.

Z4 M roadster: Game changing

If one needed evidence of how much the run-flat tires contributed to the Z4's harsh ride, BMW provided it a few years later. Although the company declared at first that no M version would be built, the 2006 model year brought the much-anticipated Z4 M Roadster. Equipped with standard high-performance tires rather than run-flats, the sportiest Z4 rode like a dream, even on a bumpy road. Its aerodynamics weren't compromised by any additional body movement, either, thanks to a deeper front air dam and a new bumper that incorporated a lower diffuser as well as cutouts for four exhaust pipes.

That allowed drivers to take full advantage of the S54 engine's performance, which improved from 315 horsepower and 251 pound feet in the Z3 M roadster to 330 horsepower and 262 pound-feet in the Z4 M Roadster. That was just three horsepower shy of what the same engine delivered in the E46 M3, a much larger and heavier car at 3,415 pounds.

Along with its S54 engine, the Z4 M Roadster also got the M3's brakes, ZF six-speed manual gearbox, and Variable M Differential Lock, and a hydro-mechanical limited-slip differential developed by BMW M and GKN Viscodrive.

In the cockpit, the Z4 M Roadster swapped the Z4's aluminum dash trim for "Carbon Leather." Leather woven to look like carbon fiber, the material had a matte finish rather than carbon's usual bright resin. The unrelenting blackness was broken only by the aluminum trim on the door handles and a bit of bright silver on the gauges. The Z4 M also got deeply bolstered Sport seats and a thick-rimmed steering wheel that connected to the front wheels via hydraulic assist rather than the Z4's much-reviled Electric Power Steering.

Most interestingly, the Z4 M Roadster got a revised hood created with technology developed for GINA. Where the Z4's hood consists of a single smooth surface, the Z4 M's adds two creases that echo the fender edges, leading the eye upward from the front of the car toward the windshield. Executed by the robotics team led by Stefan Bartscher, the creases were created by clamping the Z4's aluminum hood at the edges and holding it in space while a tool embossed the metal in two sweeping strokes.

"It put these beautiful lines on it, which no engineer knew how to predict," said Chris Bangle. "It turns out that the physiology of the metal undergoing that process does not correspond to what they thought would happen in terms of ductile forming and retraction. It was a complete surprise. It also cost maybe one-twentieth of what a stamp would have cost, and which we never would have gotten through."

Because the process was digital rather than analog, the tool made minute steps in its arc along the hood rather than rolling along the surface to create a continuous crease. "It worked in superfine steps, and when that's painted, you can see a fine set of ridges," Bangle said. "It got rejected by the paint people, but I argued that it's the signature of the tool. It's beautiful! BMW even donated one to the Pinakothek der Moderne, as an example of the first car produced with a rapid manufacturing component."

Though its appearance and performance were objectively improved, the Z4 M Roadster didn't offer the lunatic thrills of its Z3-based predecessor. On the sales floor, the Z4 M Roadster proved less successful than its predecessor. BMW produced just 2,346 examples for Europe—of which 921 were right-hand drive cars for the UK— and another 3,041 for the US. That 5,387-car total was barely one-third the number of Z3 M roadsters produced, making the Z4 M Roadster a relatively rare bird among BMWs.

"This isn't necessarily a volume car," said Dr. Göschel at the M Roadster's launch in 2006. "It's one thing to earn money, and it's another to satisfy enthusiasts. It's also a must for the brand to express its values, and a roadster historically represents BMW's brand values."

Göschel was then BMW's board member for R&D, and his assessment of the car was somewhat different two decades later. "I personally was not satisfied with the Z4 M versions," Göschel told me in 2021. "They did not have enough of their own character. We had a change in leadership at M, and [Ulrich Bruhnke] coming from AMG did not understand

M." [Bruhnke joined BMW as head of the M division in January 2003, and he resigned in January 2007.]

Despite Göschel's later criticism, plenty of enthusiasts thought the M Roadster represented BMW's values rather well. *Bimmer* magazine declared it "fast and fun, full of character and charisma. It's deeply satisfying to drive, and it's the one BMW we'd reach for if told we had just hours left on Earth in which to enjoy a motor vehicle. No question: It's simply that good."

E86 Z4 Coupe
Double-bubble blast

Just as BMW had proclaimed initially that no M version of the Z4 would be offered, so it had declared that no coupe was in the works, either. In 2006, however, the M Roadster did indeed arrive in dealer showrooms, along with a pair of Z4 coupes.

The hardtop Z4 was conceptualized at Designworks in California. "I did it with Henrik Fisker's leadership," said Anders Warming, who'd designed the Z4 roadster in 1998. "Henrik took the initiative and said, 'Let's do it!' I designed it with the premise of a 30mm wider rear track, and only as an M car. It was like a Cobra coupe, very heavy on the testosterone, and with a really aggressive stance. Part of the premise of the new taillights on the facelifted Z4 was to make the coupe feasible."

With the model completed, Warming went to Munich to see if it had a future. "We showed it to Dr. Göschel, and he liked it," Warming told me in 2021. "He especially liked the idea of doing a coupe with a fastback roofline rather than another shoe box like the Z3 coupe with the boxy back end."

The rest of the board agreed with Göschel, and the coupe was given the green light, assigned the internal development code E86. Warming returned to Designworks, while Thomas Sycha remained in Munich to guide the design for the coupe—and the Z4 facelift—into production. Sycha was able to keep the double-bubble roof intact, and it proved to be one of the most subtly compelling aspects of its design. The feature echoed not only the great Zagato race cars of the '50s and '60s, but Fisker's design for the ill-starred Z8 coupe.

Beyond the design, the project was undertaken at BMW M, first under the guidance of longtime M CEO Adolph Prommesberger and then by Ulrich Bruhnke from early 2003.

Like the Z4 M Roadster, the Coupe would borrow its drivetrain from the E46 M3. In both Z4-based cars, the magnificent S54 six delivered 330 horsepower at 7,900 rpm and 262 pound-feet at 4,900 rpm to the rear wheels via a ZF Type H six-speed manual transmission, followed by an M Differential Lock with a 3.62:1 ratio.

That drivetrain had been used on the final iterations of the Z3 M roadster and coupe, too, but the earlier cars couldn't make the most of it thanks to their relatively primitive chassis. The Z4 had a distinct advantage in that regard,

having started with the superior E46 platform rather than the earlier E36 chassis. Even as a roadster, the Z4 was nearly three times as stiff as its predecessor, and adding a roof doubled that figure again.

For comparison, consider the torsional stiffness for each car:

Z3 roadster: 5,600 Nm/degree
Z3 coupe: 16,400 Nm/degree
Z4 Roadster: 14,500 Nm/degree
Z4 Coupe: 32,000 Nm/degree

That ultra-stiff chassis allowed the team led by Gerhard Richter to tune the suspension for maximum performance. Compared to the Z4 M Roadster, the Coupe got front springs that were five percent stiffer. At the rear, the springs were progressive, starting with the same rates as the roadster while becoming much stiffer as they neared full compression. The shock and strut damping rates were set accordingly. The Z4 M Coupe also got a larger rear anti-roll bar than the roadster, one that measured 22.5mm in diameter rather than 21.5.

As on the M Roadster, Electric Power Steering was swapped for more feelsome hydraulic assist, here with the M3 CSL's sharper 14.5:1 ratio rather than the standard E46 M3's 15.4:1. (At the press launch in Spain, the rack ratios were quoted as 12.8:1 for the Z4 M Coupe, 13.7:1 for the Roadster; both numbers seem impossibly low.)

Warming's proposal for wider rear wheel track was rejected, and the figure remained unchanged at 59.7 inches. The front track, on the other hand, was widened from 58.0 to 58.5 inches for a mild reduction in understeer. The wheelbase remained identical at 98.3 inches.

More weight, slippery aero

The addition of the roof brought curb weight to 3,230 pounds, distributed equally between front and rear axles. The Z4 M Coupe was 33 pounds heavier than the Z4 M Roadster, but it compensated for its additional weight with superior aerodynamics: Its Cd of 0.35 was significantly better than the Roadster's 0.38, especially as both cars had the same 1.91-meter frontal area. The two M cars posted an identical 4.9-second time in the zero-to-60 mph dash, en route to the same electronically-limited top speed of 155 mph.

Braking came via cast-iron discs (13.7-inch front, 12.9-inch rear) and single-piston calipers borrowed from the M3 CSL. These worked well enough on the street, but they offered insufficient heat dissipation after multiple track laps. They also lacked sex appeal, especially when other manufacturers were fitting Brembo's colorful multi-piston calipers.

Eighteen-inch wheels with offset widths—8.0 inches up front, 9.0 inches at the rear—held 225/45ZR-18 and 255/40ZR-18-inch non-run flat tires, respectively. Where those had cured the M Roadster of its Z4 counterpart's harsh ride, they didn't do so to the same degree on the Coupe thanks to its stiffer suspension. Should an M Coupe driver exceed the available traction, DSC would keep the car on track by applying the brake to arrest wheelspin or other traction imbalances (like excessive yaw).

Z4 3.0si Coupe: Non-M alternative

For those who wanted a hardtop without the expense of maintaining an M car, BMW created the Z4 3.0si Coupe. Powered by the uprated version of the 2,996cc N52 Valvetronic six, the 3.0si had 255 horsepower at 6,600 rpm and 220 pound-feet at 2,700 rpm. Power was delivered to the rear wheels via a Getrag Type H six-speed manual or a ZF six-speed Steptronic automatic, paired with a standard differential with a 3.46:1 ratio. With the manual transmission, the 3.0si Coupe could scoot from zero to 60 in 5.6 seconds.

Accordingly, it had smaller brake discs (12.8 front, 11.6-inch rear) than the M car, set behind 8.0 x 17-inch wheels at all four corners.

As the "s" in 3.0si stood for Sport, the car got Sport seats and sport-tuned suspension, albeit with spring and damper rates that took the stiffness of its run-flat tires into account. It worked well on smooth pavement, but the ride proved predictably harsh over sharp-edged bumps.

Among the rarest of BMWs

The first E86 was shown to the public at Frankfurt in September 2005. Despite its identification as the Z4 Coupe Concept, the car was nearly production-ready, and the Z4 3.0si Coupe would go into production in virtually identical form to the car seen on the show stand and in the photos on this spread. In March 2006, the Z4 M Coupe was shown at Geneva, as a car destined for production rather than a concept.

Both models started rolling off the assembly line in April 2006. Like all Z3s and Z4s, the Z4 Coupes would be produced exclusively at Spartanburg, using drivetrains built in Germany and shipped to South Carolina.

The E86 was always destined to be a low-volume car, having been introduced for the Z4's last two model years. Indeed, BMW produced just 2,766 examples of the Z4 M Coupe for Europe (in left- and right-hand drive configurations), plus 1,815 for the US before the line shut down for good in August 2008. That total of 4,581 cars was far fewer than the 6,281 Z3 M coupes built, and it made the Z4 M Coupe among the rarest of M cars.

The Z4 3.0si was equally rare among series-production BMWs, with just 12,513 examples reportedly built from 2006 to 2008.

Never fully appreciated in its day, the Z4 M Coupe and its 3.0si counterpart have retained their value well nonetheless. Today, some fifteen years after their introduction, pristine, low-mileage examples trade at close to their original retail prices of $49,995 and $40,795, with "driver-class" examples selling for perhaps half that.

Z4 M Coupe: The Racer

In March 2006, BMW unveiled a racing version of the Z4 M Coupe at the Geneva auto salon. Though displayed in livery reminiscent of BMW Motorsport's white with tricolor stripes, the car wasn't intended to be a factory race car. Instead, the Z4 M Coupe was built for customers, specifically those looking for a car that could contend in the German Endurance Championship or the Nürburgring 24 Hour race. BMW suggested that the car could be eligible for "other non-European endurance series," too, but that didn't include the American Le Mans Series, which ran to rules established by the ACO for the 24 Hours of Le Mans.

As developed by BMW Motorsport, the car was equipped with a modified version of the S54 inline six-cylinder engine that displaced 3,246cc and delivered 400 horsepower to the rear wheels via a six-speed sequential gearbox with a sintered-metal clutch. Braking was via six-piston calipers that gripped 14.96-inch rotors up front, and four-piston calipers working on 12.6-inch discs at the rear. Its bodywork featured a deep, downforce-producing air dam up front, and an adjustable wing at the rear. Both front and rear fenders were widened to accommodate larger wheels and racing-spec rubber, with large outlets to expel hot air from the engine bay and brakes.

Inside, the car was stripped of its roadgoing niceties and fitted with a full roll cage, racing seats, harnesses, and a racing-spec steering wheel. As required by the regulations, the Z4 M Coupe retained elements of its stock dashboard and gauge panel, albeit with different information displayed to the driver.

Along with the Nürburgring 24 and other German endurance races, the Z4 M Coupe would race primarily in Japan. Two cars were entered in the 2008 Super Taikyu Endurance Series, raced by the Petronas Syntium team to the Super Taikyu 1 championship. Another Z4 M Coupe won the Britcar 24 Hour race at Silverstone before the car was retired at the end of 2009.

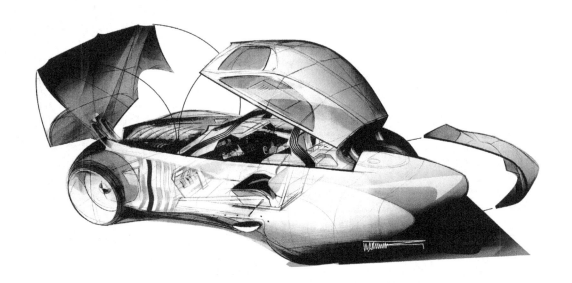

Mille Miglia Concept Coupe

In the spring of 2006, BMW revealed its most outrageous concept car yet, one that rivaled the X coupé for sheer audaciousness. Shown at the Villa d'Este concours on Italy's Lake Como, the Mille Miglia Concept Coupe paid homage to the Touring-bodied 328 coupe that had won the 1940 *Gran Premio di Brescia*, staged nearby.

Like the Z4 roadster and coupe, it was designed by Anders Warming, and it displayed his signature mix of sharp edges and evocative curves. He'd penned the car following his return to BMW after an eighteen-month sojourn at Volkswagen's Advanced Design studio from late 2003 to early 2005.

Warming says he's long been a fan of Touring Superleggera automobiles, and that he'd begun sketching 328-based cars upon his return to BMW in 2005.

"The Mille Miglia Concept happened not quite as a joke, but just for fun," Warming told me in 2021. "I was sitting around with Chris Bangle, and he asked me to lead the Advanced Design studio for BMW.

"We were joking that it would be fun to do different kinds of things with the Z4 form language, mixing up things like a Bugatti Atalante to create the Zatalante, or a Riva boat called the Ziva. Mixing the Z4 with the Mille Miglia coupe, we came up with the Zille Ziglia."

Within the context of Advanced Design, Warming had the capacity to explore all sorts of ideas, no matter how whimsical.

"We were doing a whole row of cars at Bertone in Torino, where they had the capacity for model building," he said. "We did like ten cars in plaster, then the eleventh one became the Zille Ziglia."

Renamed the Mille Miglia Concept Coupe, the car soon moved from plaster model to working concept. In Munich, the prototype engineering team led by Joachim Kolling built the concept atop an E85 Z4 Roadster chassis. Riding on 20-inch wheels, it had an identical footprint but for slightly wider front wheel tracks. Its exterior dimensions were rather different: 9.0 inches longer, mainly at the rear, 5.5 inches wider, and 1.6 inches lower than those of the Z4.

The concept was propelled by a 340-horsepower version of the Z4 M roadster's S54 six-cylinder, here with a new intake and exhaust system. Relatively unmuffled, it produced a much more evocative sound than a street-legal Z4 M Roadster or Coupe.

Its headlights were LEDs, as were the side market lights embedded in a series of strakes just aft of the front wheels. The taillight consisted of a series of LEDs that cut diagonally across the car's rear, adding a bit of the asymmetry that had defined the X coupé. "That was Chris. He put the brake light in the back," Warming said.

The sheet metal inside and out had been created with "industrial origami," a technique borrowed from the Japanese paper art and taught to the BMW prototyping team by an origami master. The 1mm thick stainless steel sheet metal itself was laser-cut to bend in precise ways, with sharp folds and a three-dimensional surface.

Inside, a full road cage protected driver and passenger inside a cabin that was as spare as any Touring-bodied racer's. Brown leather covered the seats, steering wheel, and other trim pieces, lending an organic contrast to the folded aluminum of the bodywork.

Overall, the Mille Miglia Concept Coupe was a remarkable exercise, one that explored new techniques and technologies while paying homage to BMW's racing heritage.

"Rather than make a retro-look car, we wanted to make a visual statement celebrating the past in form, interpreted with 21st-century details and made from state-of-the-art materials with state-of-the-art manufacturing techniques," Bangle told *Bimmer* magazine in 2006. "This is the car that the original [328 Coupe] sees in its dreams."

As for the Mille Miglia Concept Coupe's designer, Warming moved on from the Advanced Design studio to become BMW's head of exterior design in 2007, then head of MINI design in 2011. In 2017, he left BMW to lead the design department at the revived Borgward firm. Since 2019, he's run his own firm, Warming Design in Munich.

E89 Z4 roadster
Moving upscale

Conceived and developed during the boom years of the early 20th century, the second-generation Z4 was launched into a world still shattered by the Great Recession that began in 2007. The world economy had not yet shown much improvement when the E89 Z4 premiered at Detroit in January 2009—a tough time to launch a fairly frivolous car, especially one that had taken yet another move upscale.

Along with a host of sophisticated features and powerful engines, the new Z4 would use a folding hardtop rather than the cloth top that had served BMW's roadsters since the 1930s. Entry-level it was not.

Perhaps even more ominously, customers' tastes were changing, too. After more than a decade in the mainstream, roadsters were again a niche product. SUVs had become the overwhelming choice for day-to-day driving, particularly in the US.

Adapting to the changing marketplace, BMW Manufacturing in Spartanburg, South Carolina became a "center of competence" for X-vehicle production. Its lines were devoted exclusively to the X5, X6, X3, and eventually X7, while Z4 production moved to Regensburg, Germany.

The changes were no less dramatic where BMW's leadership was concerned. In 2006, Dr. Burkhard Göschel reached BMW's mandatory retirement age of 60. Obligated to step down as board member for R&D, Göschel left BMW for the chairmanship of Magna International, the giant Canadian corporation that had built the first-generation X3 under contract for BMW.

Göschel's replacement was Dr. Klaus Draeger, who joined BMW in 1985 after earning his doctorate in engineering. Draeger worked primarily in purchasing prior to 2004, when he became responsible for body development of BMW's large cars (5, 6, and 7 Series). By all accounts a competent and exceptionally kind man, Draeger nonetheless had different priorities than Göschel, emphasizing quality, technical sophistication, and design over elements like sharp handling and driving fun.

Elsewhere on the board, Dr. Helmut Panke succeeded Prof. Joachim Milberg as chairman. A nuclear physicist by training, Panke had been at BMW since 1982. He became chairman of BMW of North America in 1993, and in 1996 he joined the board of management with responsibility first for human resources, then

finance. Upon Milberg's retirement in 2002, Panke was elected chairman.

Designed by women, inside and out

Though Chris Bangle was coming to the end of his term as head of BMW Design, his tenure included the entirety of E89 Z4 development. Here, he was instrumental in overseeing the first series-production car designed by female designers: Juliane Blasi and Nadia Arnaout.

"I'm pretty sure it's the first, and maybe the only production car ever, designed inside and out by women, and I'm pretty goddamn proud of that," Bangle told me in 2021. "It took a long time to make that happen."

The BMW board tended to play down that aspect of the E89's design, however, which Bangle said was "a sign of the culture of BMW that who did the car made absolutely no difference to them. Two women? Oh, that's nice."

Bangle praised Blasi's exterior design, which he said made the car "exude sexiness." A graduate of the Transportation Design program at Pforzheim University, Blasi (opposite, below) was 26 years old when she joined BMW in 2003. In 2005, she was sent from Munich to Southern California on a six-month exchange program at DesignworksUSA. It turned out to be the perfect environment in which to create a new roadster.

"California was of course influencing the atmosphere in which I was sketching, and my mood, because there was sun all the time and I had a Z4 to drive around," Blasi told me in 2008. "It was just a feeling of fun, driving along the coast, and I was really inspired."

Where the car's character was concerned, Blasi had her own ideas about how the Z4 should evolve. "I wanted to give the car a bit more maturity, and to bring even more emotion into the car and its surfaces. The hardtop also gave the car a completely different look."

Indeed it did, and in a good way. Unlike the folding hardtops of a decade earlier, the E89's was compact, allowing the car to retain its sexy proportions even while incorporating this "luxury" feature. "The engineers had done miles of work between the E51 and the E89, as had the suppliers," Bangle said. "At Design, Gerd Friedrichs' work to get the initial package right is absolutely essential, and so is that of Pascal Tanghe, who worked on the E93 3 Series' folding hardtop. There are a lot of unsung heroes in this process."

Not coincidentally, BMW's Regensburg plant also produced the E93 3 Series cabriolet, allowing these two folding-hardtop automobiles to be built in the same factory.

Like the E85 Z4—and the 327 coupe of the 1930s—the E89's design features a continuous line that unites the body and leads the eye across its surfaces. "It was important that the car not have front, side, and rear, but a design that flows over the whole car," Blasi said. "That's why all the lines start from the front, at the emblem, and either go over the side or over the roof and end at the trunk."

The lines that pass over the car's roof perform a function that's more than just graphic. They also create a Zagato-style "double bubble" roof, a feature incorporated on nearly all of BMW's two-seat coupes.

Perhaps most interesting of all is the line that begins at the inside corner of the headlight and flows across the side of the car, integrating the door handle on its way to the rear wheel. Such details are technically difficult and expensive to execute, and they aren't easy to get through to production. Designers have to make a strong case for their inclusion, which Blasi did with the advocacy of people including Bangle.

During her time at Designworks, Blasi made more than just a car. She also made a friend, Nadya Arnaout (next page, below), whose driver-oriented cockpit won the Z4's interior design competition.

"Our models were sitting behind one another when we were in the beginning stages, and we didn't know that they'd end up together," Arnaout told me in 2008. "We had an influence on each other, because we saw certain form language and said, 'That's cool!' When these two designs were chosen for production, we were happy because we were already in synch."

Arnaout earned a diploma in Industrial Design at the *Hochschule für Gestaltung*, an art and

design university in Offenbach am Main in 1995, then completed a BS in Product and Industrial Design at Art Center in Pasadena in 2000. She joined DesignworksUSA upon graduating, and she was working primarily on Nokia cell phones when her design was chosen for the interior of the Concept CS. Shown at Shanghai in 2007, the Concept CS previewed a new design direction for BMW's large sedans, and it also foretold the four-door Grand Coupes that would follow.

Arnaout designed her CS interior concurrently with Karim Habib's exterior, and it was a perfect match for the sheet metal. "The interior takes some of its shapes from the exterior. You shouldn't open the door and enter a different world," Arnaout told me in 2007. Indeed, the interior flowed readily from the exterior, enveloping its occupants in elegantly curving and overlapping forms that evoked origami.

Unfortunately, when the Concept CS went into production as the F01 7 Series, it had a much more conservative interior than Arnaout had designed. All was not lost, however. The CS's themes carried over into the E89 Z4, even though the smaller car had a distinct identity and purpose. "The overall dimensions are very different, but I wanted to keep the driver in focus," Arnaout said. "I was also very interested to have a strong asymmetry in the center console, which also has parallels to the CS. I wanted to have contrast between the driver and passenger, giving the passenger more comfort and luxury, to let them sit back and enjoy the ride."

Arnaout also wanted to emphasize the Z4's newfound spaciousness, a goal facilitated by the folding hardtop and larger overall dimensions. On the dash and center console, the now *de rigeur* iDrive controller allowed the concept to be realized with little clutter and a minimum of buttons and switches.

The Fun Car in adulthood

Perhaps inevitably, the roadster had grown along with every other BMW. Consider this trajectory: When the six-cylinder Z3 2.8 launched in 1997, it weighed 2,844 pounds and rolled on a 96.3-inch wheelbase, within an overall length of 158.5 inches. In 2002, the E85 Z4 3.0i that replaced it weighed 2,899 pounds, had a 98.2-inch wheelbase and an overall length of 161.1 inches. In 2009, the E89 Z4 3.0i weighed 3,241 pounds, with a 98.3-inch wheelbase and an overall length of 166.9 inches.

The Z4 was smaller than an E46 3 Series, but it was no longer truly small in roadster terms.

"The growth in the Z4's dimensions reflects a change in its mission," wrote *Bimmer* magazine following the car's launch in Spain. "It's no longer quirky and fun like the Z3, nor is it edgy and weird like the E85 Z4. In E89 guise, it's grown in to responsible adulthood, with a good deal of sophistication. It's the most technically astute BMW roadster ever built, yet it hasn't become boring in the process. Not at all."

The car debuted as the Z4 sDrive 35i, the new nomenclature referring to the model, "standard" aka rear-wheel drive, and the engine configuration. The "35i" was bit misleading, as the car was powered by the 2,979cc N54 six-cylinder. Combining twin turbochargers with Valvetronic and Double VANOS, the N54 put out 300 horsepower at 4,800 rpm and 300 pound-feet from 1,400 to 5,000 rpm—almost as much as the S54 six in the outgoing Z4 M Roadster and Coupe.

The engine was paired with a Getrag Type D six-speed manual as standard, which allowed the Z4 to reach 60 mph from a dead stop in just 5.1 seconds. With the optional six-speed Dual Clutch Transmission, the ZF 436 that replaced SMG, it was faster still, needing just 5.0 seconds to reach the same benchmark. Acceleration was aided by Launch Control, a technology borrowed from Formula One that was really fun to use, albeit a bit hard on tires. (No torque converter automatic was available.)

The drivetrain's performance helped ameliorate the lack of a Z4 M, and so did sport-tuned electronics led by Dynamic Drive Control. Standard on all models, DDC allowed the driver to toggle between maps for steering assist, throttle response, DCT shift speed, and the threshold of intervention for Dynamic Stability Control. Further adjustability could be obtained with the optional Adaptive M Suspension, included with Sport Package along with sport

seats, etc. Adaptive M Suspension lowered the car's ride height by 0.4 inch, and it also allowed the driver to select between Normal, Sport, and Sport+ settings for damper stiffness.

Choosing Normal helped alleviate the run-flat tires' harsh ride. Sport and Sport+ allowed the driver to take full advantage of the E89 Z4's capable chassis, in which lateral stiffness had improved by about 15% over the E85.

Beyond adjustability, the suspension reflected a new tuning philosophy in the post-Göschel era. The individual in charge of R&D has an extraordinary influence over the outcome of BMW's automobiles, and every board member to hold that position really puts his stamp on the cars' character. As BMW chassis engineer Heinz Krusche told me in 2009, Göschel often preferred the stiffest ride bearable. New R&D chief Draeger directed the engineers toward softer springs, stiffer damper settings, and fine-tuned bump stops to achieve an optimum balance of comfort and control on the obligatory run-flat tires. Combined with DDC and Adaptive M Suspension, the new settings proved effective. The car felt fluid and smooth in Normal mode, sporty and aggressive in Sport+.

Steering feel improved greatly, too. The E89 still used Electric Power Steering, but the system had improved considerably over seven years of development. BMW had relocated the power assist from the steering column to sit alongside it, which provided more "feel" and feedback. It also made the steering feel more direct, even though the ratio was higher than in the E85 (14.4:1 instead of 14.2).

A big step forward, not least in price

On the whole, the E89 Z4 represented a big step forward for BMW's two-seater in terms of sophistication, and its price would reflect that improvement. Base MSRP for the Z4 35i rose to $51,650, roughly double what the original Z3 had cost just 13 years earlier. (Building the car in Germany didn't help, as the *Deutschmark*'s replacement by the Euro was inflationary in itself, even before tariffs were applied.)

Initially, the price of the Z4 35i was offset slightly by the more affordable Z4 sDrive 30i,

which retailed for a still rather spendy $45,570. The car was powered by a 2,996cc version of the naturally-aspirated N52 six-cylinder, which featured Valvetronic, Double VANOS, and a three-stage induction system to deliver 255 horsepower at 6,600 rpm and 220 pound-feet at 2,600 rpm. Acceleration was a still-respectable 5.6 seconds from zero to 60 with the Getrag Type I manual, or 6.0 seconds with the optional GM-built Steptronic automatic. No DSC option would be offered on the Z4 30i.

Following the car's mid-cycle facelift for 2011, the N52 was replaced by the turbocharged 1,999cc N20 four-cylinder. Although the engine was smaller, its output was comparable: 240 horsepower at 5,00 rpm, 258 pound-feet from 1,250-4,800 rpm in the Z4 28i sDrive. The smaller engine delivered excellent fuel economy, but it didn't bring a cheaper car, as the Z4 28i carried a base price of $49,525.

At the other end of the price spectrum—$61,925, to be precise—BMW upped the sportiness of the top-flight Z4 by giving it the most powerful N54 built and adding an "s" to its model name. The Z4 35is came standard with the new M Sport Package and Adaptive M Suspension, but the real story was its engine. Changes to the electronics allowed the turbocharger to go into "overboost mode" when the throttle was pinned to the floor, increasing torque output from 332 pound-feet to 370 for several seconds. (Horsepower registered a stellar 335 at 5,800 rpm)

Zero to 60 fell to just 4.8 seconds, but the real benefit could be felt on a track, where overboost provided incredible acceleration and eliminated the need for an extra shift in certain situations. Paired with a new seven-speed DCT, the N54 delivered superlative performance. (Later, it would be shared by the 1 Series M Coupe, a legendary and limited-production two-door.)

It was also a blast to drive. As *Bimmer* reported in 2010 following a multi-car test of BMW's sportiest cars, "It's agile and lighthearted when you aren't pushing hard, and it's challenging to drive when you *are* pushing hard. Its ultra-short wheelbase—just 98.3 inches— renders it a tad unstable, a fact that's compounded under

acceleration by its lack of a limited slip differential. [The car had an electronically simulated LSD.] In addition, the car's DTC setting is fairly liberal, allowing a lot of slip angle before it reels in the oversteer. The Z4 35is is expensive, but it needs nothing beyond its base specification to make for maximum fun. Bring your best driving skills and let it rip."

Predictably, however, the newly upscale Z4 found fewer takers than the fun-loving and affordable Z3, or its E85 predecessor. BMW produced some 118,444 examples, of which 21,710 were imported to the US.

That total represented just two-thirds the number of E85s, but it was still respectable, especially for a car launched at the beginning of a global financial crisis that persisted for years. Buying a roadster indicates a sort of carefree optimism, and that mood was in short supply as the Great Recession wore on.

So was enthusiasm for the roadster segment in general, even within BMW. After eight years with the E89, BMW seemed unlikely to build a third-generation Z4 after the last E89 left Regensburg in August 2018. That it did was a stroke of luck, and it relied on an unexpected and unusual partnership.

As for those responsible for the E89, Dr. Klaus Draeger retired from the BMW board of management in 2012, succeeded by Dr. Herbert Diess. Juliane Blasi went on to design the Vision ConnectedDrive concept seen on page 144; she remains at BMW Design. Nadya Arnaout left BMW Designworks in 2009 to become lead interior designer on the Tesla Model S; since 2011, she's been Fisker Automotive's director of interior design.

BMW design chief Chris Bangle had planned to stay in the role for no more than 15 years, but he remained at BMW for 17 and announced his retirement shortly after the E89 Z4 debuted in Detroit. He'd be replaced by Adrian van Hooydonk, whose E65 7 Series had debuted to considerable controversy in 2001, followed by his equally disruptive E63 6 Series. Van Hooydonk remains as head of BMW Design to this day, having overseen a generational leap forward for the department.

Z4 GTE/LM: Unlikely racer

When the E92 M3 GT was retired at the end of the 2012 season of American Le Mans Series racing, its two-door successor wasn't due until 2014. Even then, the new M4 wasn't sure to replace the M3 as BMW's premiere GT racer in North America, where BMW Motorsport had been campaigning the M3 since 1986. Further complicating matters, the ALMS was set to merge with its Grand-Am rival for 2014, bringing a new United SportsCar Championship and a new rule book.

To bridge the gap, BMW of North America turned to the Z4 GT3, introduced as a customer racer in 2010. The car was well-proven on the endurance circuit: It won the 24 Hours of Dubai in 2010, then finished second at the 24 Hours of Spa in 2011. It also scored numerous race wins in the FIA GT3 and Blancpain Endurance series, as well as the Japanese GT3000 title.

Adapting the GT3 to ALMS rules proved more difficult than one might expect, however. Although the series permitted BMW Motorsport to use the 4.4-liter P65 V8 engine rather than a four- or six-cylinder like that of the production Z4, the car's body shape made it difficult to take advantage of all 480 horsepower.

Specifically, the car's steep rear window and short decklid created pocket of dead air instead of a clean flow over the rear wing. BMW labored mightily to correct it, but sometimes that resulted in too much downforce, sometimes in none at all. At Daytona in 2013, the car ran with its rear wing set flat, resulting in lift rather than downforce to ensure adequate top speed on the banking.

What BMW could do with the rear wing was limited by ALMS rules, which didn't let BMW hang the wing out as far off the back of the car as would have been ideal. To make it as effective as possible required considerable use of BMW's wind tunnel in Munich, as well as Computational Fluid Dynamics. "It was a really tough job to make a GTE car out of a GT3 car," said BMW Motorsport Director Jens Marquardt.

The Z4's rear fenders and diffuser also came in for considerable revision, again in an effort to optimize air flow around the rear wing. Even the mirrors were revised, becoming larger and gaining a new shape to redirect airflow from the sides of the car to the rear wing.

Even after all of the revisions, the Z4 GTE was estimated to make around 30 percent less downforce than its GT3 counterpart. Per the rulebook, it also lost ABS and DSC, both of which would have been nice to have on such a short-wheelbase car.

Despite the challenges, BMW Motorsport's efforts to transform the Z4 into a race winner eventually did just that. The car won two races in 2013, and the BMW Team Rahal Letterman Lanigan finished second to Corvette in the final standings.

Renamed the Z4 GTLM for 2014, the BMW Motorsport cars failed to win a single race in the USCC's premiere GT class, but the privately-entered Turner Motorsport Z4s ended up taking home the GTD championship.

For 2015, the Z4 GTLM benefited from yet more modifications as well as Balance of Performance adjustments from the racing stewards. The Z4 GTLM won three races, while the team and its drivers finished second to Porsche in their respective championships.

And with that, BMW Motorsport concluded its Z4 experiment. Even if it retired without winning a title, the car had proved immensely popular with race fans, who loved rooting for this underdog BMW against the race-bred Porsches, Ferraris, and Corvettes that formed their primary opposition. Gloriously mechanical and captivatingly different, the Z4 recalled BMW's mid-'70s run in IMSA with the CSL, racing at a technical disadvantage but coming away with credible victories and making plenty of friends along the way.

BMW Zagato Coupe and Roadster

Throughout this book, I've referred to the "Zagato-style" double-bubble roof on the Z07 concept's removable hardtop, the E86 Z4 M Coupe, and the E89 Z4. This distinctive feature originated in the 1950s, when Italian coachbuilder Zagato needed to create more headroom for a helmeted racing driver without raising the car's entire roofline.

BMW's designers clearly had a thing for Zagato-style roofs, and in 2012 they got one straight from the source. In an unusual collaboration, BMW partnered with Zagato to create the BMW Zagato Coupe and Roadster, which were shown to the public at the Villa d'Este and Pebble Beach concours, respectively.

Throughout its history, BMW had commissioned work from Italian *carrozzerie* and designers including Touring, Giovanni Michelotti, Bertone, and Italdesign. Ex-Zagato designer Ercole Spada had penned the E32 7 Series and E34 5 Series while employed by BMW in Munich, but this project represented the first collaboration between BMW and Zagato itself.

Starting with an E89 Z4, Zagato chief designer Norihiko Harada (at far right in photo opposite) penned the original sketches—first the coupe, and then the roadster that followed as a bonus. From there, Harada collaborated with BMW Design's Erik Goplen (far left) and Karim Habib (center), among others, to bring the cars to life as an embodiment of both BMW and Zagato brand values.

BMW and Zagato share roots in the airplane industry, BMW as a maker of aircraft engines since 1916 and Zagato as a maker of planes since 1919. That set Zagato apart from coachbuilders who got their start making horse-drawn carriages, said current chairman Andrea Zagato, grandson of founder Ugo Zagato. "They are a little bit ornamental, and we are not ornamental at all," Zagato told me in 2012. "Plus, Milan was under the Austrian Empire, so we are much more influenced by German design than French— Rationalism and Functionalism, the necessary beauty, minimal design."

Having a common culture helped push the project forward, and so did a willingness to collaborate completely. "The idea was to match the DNA of BMW with the DNA of Zagato to get a final result that is in harmony, and is the sum of the two DNA," Zagato said.

Habib agreed, but emphasized the need for the coachbuilder's style to be at the fore. "The first time I came down to Milan, I said it was very important that the cars are Zagato, with the Kamm tail, the double-bubble roof. For me, the project made sense when it's really a Zagato."

"But we didn't want to stay in the existing design territory or design language," said Harada. "Zagato tried to go a little beyond the usual design approach, and maybe BMW also."

"This project was everybody bringing their best ideas and skills to the table," said Goplen, then creative director at BMW DesignworksUSA.

That includes the craftspeople in Milan who disassembled the unit-body BMW Z4 and re-bodied it with hand-built aluminum bodywork. That work was done in collaboration between Zagato project leader Marco Pedracini and BMW design technicians Jürgen Steinle and Jürgen Greil. Also in Milan, the interiors were given Zagato's sporty but luxurious treatment by Marella Rivolta-Zagato and BMW's Marc Girard.

Once completed, the BMW Zagato Coupe was shown at Villa d'Este in May 2012, the BMW Zagato Roadster at Pebble Beach that August. The cars were well received, raising hopes that they might see production.

"If we can get this car into limited production," Habib told me in 2012, "the greatest achievement is that we can take the brand into a realm where it hasn't been before. To get the collectors who buy cars that are worth millions into a BMW roadster or coupe would be a great thing."

Alas, it wasn't meant to be, and the cars remained one-off concepts. So, too, did the BMW Pininfarina Gran Lusso Coupe of 2013, a gorgeously understated car based on the V12-powered 7 Series. Both collaborations suggested new possibilities for BMW, however, and they moved the game forward inside and out.

i8 Roadster
From Vision to reality

When BMW's Vision EfficientDynamics concept (opposite, top) rolled onstage at the 2009 Frankfurt auto show, it came as a total surprise. The car was so strikingly beautiful that the assembled journalists let out a collective gasp of excitement. The response was so overwhelmingly positive that BMW had no choice but to build it.

Designed by Mario Majdanzic under the supervision of Anders Warming as head of exterior design, the Vision would eventually become the i8. First, however, it proceeded through several concept phases while BMW engineers and designers worked to make it a production-car reality.

This required more time than usual, as the car's powertrain had been conceived as a diesel-electric hybrid that proved unworkable in series production. A gasoline-electric hybrid took its place, but it took time to develop to the appropriate level of performance. The car's bodywork, too, needed to be simplified for production, and to pass international safety standards that precluded the use of all-glass doors.

The wait would be long, but it wasn't boring thanks to a steady stream of concept cars that kept enthusiasts engaged. Two of those concepts were roadsters: the Vision ConnectedDrive shown at Geneva in early 2011, and the 328 Hommage displayed at Villa d'Este later that spring. Both raised hopes for a Vision-based roadster; alas, none materialized alongside the i8 Concept Coupe shown at Frankfurt that September.

And then, rather unexpectedly, BMW revealed the i8 Spyder in April 2012. This car was especially promising, as it was essentially the Vision EfficientDynamics refined and simplified for production. Alas, while the production i8 coupe reached the public in April 2014, its roadster counterpart wouldn't be confirmed for production until 2016. Even then, the i8 Roadster (opposite, below) wouldn't arrive in dealer showrooms for another two years.

We'll look at the i8 Roadster in a few pages. First, let's examine the concepts that preceded its arrival.

Vision ConnectedDrive

The first Vision-inspired roadster concept was the Vision ConnectedDrive (left), a stylish two-seater shown at Geneva in March 2011.

With an exterior by Juliane Blasi, the Vision ConnectedDrive consolidated a number of recent BMW design themes, including those expressed on GINA and Blasi's own E89 Z4. It also nodded to the Z07 concept of 1997 with a pair of aerofins behind the cockpit. The car featured striking aerodynamics, with transparent panels that gave liquidity to the shape while revealing the car's functions in a dramatic new ways.

Although it was spectacular to look at, the car's real purpose was to highlight forthcoming changes to the driver interface. The interior by Robert Hlinovsky featured cockpit lighting that could change colors to suit the driver's mood, plus a host of new features developed at BMW's Technology Office in Palo Alto, California. (It's now located in Mountain View). Many of those features have since become reality, including head-up displays with driver-selectable data points, integration of smartphone data (addresses, calendar, music) and communication functions with the car's on-board computer, advanced GPS data, and driver assistance features like crash detection warning and intervention. Some of the concept's more fanciful aspects have yet to be implemented, but today's information-rich touchscreens were largely foretold by the Vision ConnectedDrive—for good or ill.

"The concept emphasizes infotainment over driving, reflecting the priorities of a new generation of automobile consumers," wrote *Bimmer* magazine in 2011. "Its very existence seems a tacit acknowledgment that a car's primary purpose is no longer to deliver driving fun or even transportation, but a form of entertainment distinct from both."

If that assessment sounded pessimistic, *Bimmer* found redemption in the car's styling, which expressed the essence of an emotionally satisfying roadster experience.

328 Hommage: Retro only on the surface

To commemorate the 75th anniversary of the historic Nürburgring victory for Ernst Henne and the 328 roadster, BMW Design created the 328 Hommage. Beyond its historical allusions, the car was an evolution of the Vision ConnectedDrive, which premiered at Geneva shortly before the 328 Hommage was unveiled before the start of the Mille Miglia Storica in Brescia, Italy in May 2011.

Where the Vision CD represented the ultimate expression of modernity, the 328 Hommage mixed high-tech materials and modern styling with traditional features like leather hood straps and perforated wheels. Designed by Christopher Weil, its bodywork was rendered not in aluminum or steel but carbon fiber, the quintessential lightweight material of the 21st century. The fabric's weave is visible within the clear resin, giving depth to the car's finish.

The chassis, too, was built of carbon fiber, with high side sills that allowed the 328 Hommage to go without doors, just like the prototype 328 raced by Henne at the Nürburgring.

Like the exterior, the cockpit was rife with allusions to BMW's classic racer even as it shared the ultra-modern form of the Vision ConnectedDrive. Both interiors were designed by Robert Hlinovsky; for the 328 Hommage, Hlinovsky swapped exotic lighting and high-tech gadgetry for warm brown leather, satin-finish aluminum, and traditional gauges ahead of the steering wheel. Completing the racing allusions, a pair of rally-style stopwatches were mounted on the dash, just ahead of the passenger/navigator.

From Italy, the 328 Hommage went to California, where it would be shown at Legends of the Autobahn and Pebble Beach that summer. Everywhere it went, the 328 Hommage captivated onlookers with its unique blend of vintage and modern styling, as well as its promise of exciting new roadsters to come. Alas, it would be seven more years before BMW introduced the i8 Roadster.

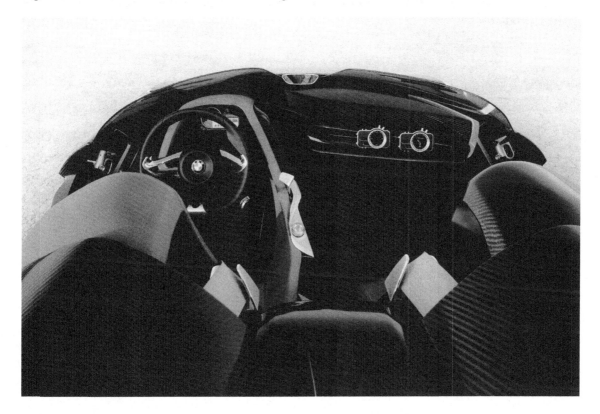

i8 Roadster: Long time coming

When the i8 Roadster finally became available for the 2018 model year, the i8 had just two years left to run. The i8 Roadster would be short-lived, but it was strikingly beautiful, perhaps even more so than the i8 Coupe.

The i8 Roadster's exterior was designed by Robert Forrest. Born in England, Forrest earned his undergraduate degree in Transport Design at Coventry University before completing a Master's in Vehicle Design at the Royal College of Art in 2005. He started his career at Honda in Tokyo before returning to England in 2010 to take a job with Lotus. He joined BMW in 2013, designing the exteriors of BMW's production i3 and i3S before penning the i8 Roadster. (Forrest is seen at left in the photo on page 151, delivering one of the first i8 Roadsters to an unidentified customer.)

Forrest gave the i8 Roadster's rear deck a fascinating variant on the Vision ConnectedDrive's aerofins. Atop both fins, a body-colored cap flowed elegantly from the cockpit to the taillights, echoing the coupe's roofline while creating drama all its own. More dramatic still were the car's doors. Like those of the i8 Coupe, they opened scissors-style, allowing occupants to enter or exit even in relatively narrow spaces. Once inside, they were comfortably ensconced in a multi-layered interior, one of BMW's best.

Opening the doors also revealed the i8's carbon fiber chassis, visible in the hefty door sills and elsewhere. The carbon fiber strands were produced in Moses Lake, Washington, then shipped to Leipzig, Germany to be woven into mats and formed into chassis parts at an all-new plant devoted solely to i-car production. Highlighting the project's zero-emissions nature, all of the necessary energy was produced by on-site wind turbines.

Like the i8 Coupe, the i8 Roadster used a hybrid gas-electric powertrain, upgraded for 2018 with a lithium ion battery that could store 11.6 kwH of energy rather than just 7.1 kw/H, for a maximum all-electric range of 32 miles. The car's battery rode under the floor, placed along the longitudinal axis to help centralize the car's mass for optimum handling.

Up front, an electric motor delivered 143 horsepower at 4,800 rpm and 184 pound-feet to the front wheels through a two-speed automatic gearbox. At the rear, a gasoline-burning 1,499cc three-cylinder engine (with turbocharging, Valvetronic and direct fuel injection) delivered 231 horsepower from 5,800-6,000 rpm and 236 pound-feet at 3,700 rpm to the rear wheels via a six-speed automatic gearbox with a manual shifting option. Together, the two power sources combined for a maximum of 374 horsepower, delivered to all four wheels.

Both i8 models rode on a 110.2-inch wheelbase, with track widths of 64.7 inches front and 67.8 inches rear. To reduce rolling resistance and improve aerodynamics, the 7.0 and 7.5 x 20-inch wheels and tires were mounted with relatively narrow 195/50R-20 front and 215/45R-20 tires, with more grip than those sizes would suggest.

Thanks to its abundance of carbon fiber and other lightweight materials, the i8 Roadster tipped the scales at 3,509 pounds—quite light for a modern BMW with a giant battery in its floor. Even though its drivetrain specifications weren't earth-shattering, it could make the zero-to-62 mph dash in a respectable 4.6 seconds.

It wasn't quite the supercar that some enthusiasts hoped for, but at $164,295 it cost far less than faster hybrids from Porsche, Ferrari, and McLaren. Like those cars, the i8 Roadster would be a rare sight on the road, constituting just 3,884 cars of the 20,465 i8s produced at BMW's Leipzig plant from 2014 to 2019. Of that total, 6,776 were sold in the US.

Though the compact i3 remained in production through 2021, BMW had already moved away from cars with exotic carbon-fiber construction. The i sub-brand continues to deliver battery-electric automobiles with more conventional construction and design, while BMW also offers gasoline-electric hybrid versions of its 3 Series and X5. These once-alternative powertrains are now thoroughly mainstream, bringing new levels of flexibility and energy efficiency to BMW's most popular automobiles.

G29 Z4 roadster
Thank you, Toyota!

As the final sales tally for the E89 Z4 indicated, the roadster segment was in steep decline as the 21st century wore on. The expected sales volume could no longer justify the expense to design and develop a third-generation Z4, and BMW was planning to let the model line expire in 2018. That is, until a fortuitous partnership with Toyota allowed the model to continue.

It began in 2011, when BMW and Toyota agreed to collaborate on "next-generation environment-friendly technologies," including research on lithium-ion batteries. As part of the same agreement, BMW would supply Toyota with the 1.6- and 2.0-liter turbodiesel engines that the Japanese company needed to compete successfully in Europe.

In 2012, BMW and Toyota expanded the agreement with a new memorandum of understanding. Formalized in 2013, it included joint development of a hydrogen fuel cell system, standardization of the associated hydrogen infrastructure, and collaboration on lithium-air battery technology. More intriguing were its provisions for "joint development of lightweight technologies for vehicle bodies using cutting-edge materials such as reinforced composites,"

and "joint development of architecture and components for a future sports vehicle."

Five years later, that future sports vehicle had arrived. In August 2017, BMW showed the Concept Z4 Roadster at the Pebble Beach Concours in California. Although it was called a concept, it was akin to the Z4 Concept Coupe in previewing a forthcoming production model, in this case the G29 Z4 roadster.

According to the press release, the Concept Z4 was "sporty and progressive, encapsulating the BMW Group's vision of a modern roadster." That vision included the familiar long hood, short deck, and set-back greenhouse, executed in less-familiar ways.

"The BMW Concept Z4 expresses the new BMW design language from all perspectives and in all details," said BMW Design chief Adrian van Hooydonk. "From the dynamic-looking front to the striking flanks to the clean-cut tail end: a few lines and the subtle interplay between surfaces are enough to generate a sense of power and emotion."

The Z4's exterior was designed by Calvin Luk, an Australian who studied Industrial Design at the University of Sydney before completing his

BMW Design

degree in Transportation Design at Art Center in Pasadena 2008. He'd interned at BMW Design in 2006, and at Fiat in 2007, then joined BMW's Advanced Design studio following his graduation. In 2011, he won BMW's internal design competition to create the F48 X1, as well as that of the F20 1 Series facelift in 2013. Simultaneously, he was also penning the winning design for the G01 X3, which wrapped up just in time for Luk to design the G29 Z4.

Having designed so many cars within a short period of time, Luk put his stamp on the current BMWs of this era much as Joji Nagashima did in the mid-1990s, or Anders Warming at the turn of the century. Like those designers, he updated BMW's aesthetics while maintaining continuity with its past.

"The Z4 was inspired by the Z8 at the front end," Luk told Australia's *Car Advice* in 2019. "It's got low, wide kidneys, and higher-set headlamps that peel over the front wheel arches. The headlamps are unique: two icon lights, vertically organized. It's the only BMW that does this. On the side, it's got one very clear and precise line stretching from front to rear, which underscores the clamshell hood and drives the sculpture on the side of the body."

The front bumper area is dominated by large intakes. "It should look like it's attacking the ground in front," Luk said.

That it does, but getting the front executed properly wasn't easy. As Luk told *Autocar UK*, "Every project has unique challenges, but the front tends to be the most problematic because of the required crash structures. We got the kidneys as low as possible, but we probably would have put them even lower if it weren't for other considerations.

At the sides, prominent air outlets are followed by integrated side skirts that offer aerodynamic stability and channel air toward the rear while also guiding the eye toward the car's powerful haunches.

Luk wanted the Z4's visuals to convey strong emotions, which he says are part of the whole roadster experience. "It's really thrilling to drive an open-top two-seater," he told *Car Advice*. "You feel everything: the road, the environment.

It's a multi-sensory experience, in which you not only see and hear but smell everything that's going on. A roadster should be the epitome of the Ultimate Driving Machine."

Epitomizing that passion was made a little easier thanks to BMW's decision to abandon the E89's folding hardtop for a conventional cloth top. A cloth top is lighter, of course, which aids performance, and it's also easier to package, since the roof and its attendant mechanisms are more compact than metal panels.

Aft of the roof, the rear of the car carries further allusions to the Z8. There, slightly L-shaped taillights are reminiscent of the thin neon lights that graced the Z8's rear, giving the Z4 a similarly futuristic pair of eyes above a carbon-fiber diffuser.

A sculptural interior

The Concept Z4's interior displayed a similarly sculptural design by Florian Sieve. While studying Transportation Design at Pforzheim University from 2004-2008, Sieve interned at Porsche Design and BMW Advanced Design; his work at the latter led to a full-time position after completing his degree.

In 2014, Sieve's interior concept was chosen for production in the G01 X3, his first project alongside Luk. He'd also design the G02 X4 interior, as well as the G29 Z4.

In the roadster, Sieve's interior complements Luk's sheet metal perfectly. As BMW's press release declared, "The kinship between the interior and exterior of the BMW Concept Z4 is evident in both forms and color scheme. The design language of the interior takes the powerful, three-dimensional character of the exterior and adds another voice to the dynamic chorus. Much of the interior adopts the color of the car body, creating a clear visual link between the interior and exterior. Only a classy chrome trim strip provides separation."

In the grand BMW tradition, the G29's interior is a workplace for driving, putting everything the driver needs within easy reach or view while minimizing distractions. The central touchscreen and HVAC/audio controls are angled toward the driver, while the central console includes

the bare minimum of buttons and switches beyond the iDrive controller.

The interior was designed to keep the driver cocooned in a "pure-of-purpose driving environment with a pronounced 'cone of vision,' where the steering wheel as well as the surrounding black surfaces appear to be surging forward and, in so doing, accentuate the cabin's powerful driver focus."

The controls were grouped into "function islands," and trim was kept minimal. "Indeed, it is instead the classy [there's that ridiculous word again!] materials, carefully applied polished chrome accents and swish, hexagonal laser-cut motifs in the seats that do most to create the interior's exclusive ambiance. Carbon-fiber door sill finishers and embossed asymmetrical logos in the seats and instrument panel set the seal on the interior's sporting profile."

Collaboration, and CLAR

In August 2018, the production Z4 followed the Concept Z4 Roadster with a premiere at Pebble Beach. Shown as the Z4 M40i, it would arrive in dealer showrooms in early March 2019 as a Z4 30i, with its M Performance counterpart becoming available shortly thereafter.

Unlike BMW's earlier roadsters, the G29 Z4 wouldn't be offered in coupe form. That body style is the province of Toyota, whose Supra two-seat hardtop was developed by BMW alongside the Z4. The two cars are mechanically identical but for suspension tuning and other details, with styling from their respective design departments.

Both cars are built in Austria by Magna Steyr, a division of Magna International and one of the world's largest manufacturers of vehicles under contract. Magna Steyr built BMW's first-generation X3 from 2003 to 2010, and began building BMW's 5 Series sedans in 2017.

The Z4 (and by extension the Supra) rides on BMW's CLAR platform, introduced in 2015. CLAR stands for Cluster Architecture, and it's described as a modular platform constructed of steel and aluminum, with magnesium and carbon fiber optional for certain elements. It can accommodate a variety of propulsion sources—internal combustion engine, mild hybrid, plug-in hybrid, or even battery-electric—delivered to the rear wheels, or all four. It's meant for mid-size and larger automobiles, with BMW's small cars built on the front-wheel drive UKL platform.

As all of that indicates, BMW is engineering a new level of flexibility into its development process. No longer does each car have its own platform, nor is each platform engineered for a specific powertrain. Instead, BMW uses just two basic platforms, adapting each one to suit the needs of the vehicle in question. In turn, this gives customers a wider variety of options, allowing them to mix and match cars and powertrains depending on their needs and desires.

That engineering philosophy was championed by Dr. Klaus Fröhlich, who succeeded Herbert Diess as BMW's board member for R&D in December 2014. (Diess had served on the BMW board for just two years when he departed for the chairmanship of Volkswagen, and his influence wasn't as profound as that of his predecessors or his successor.)

Like Burkhard Göschel, Fröhlich was a driving enthusiast par excellence. Born in Soest, Germany in 1960, he earned his mechanical engineering degree at Rhine-Westfalian Technical University in Aachen in 1987. Fröhlich joined BMW immediately after graduation, and by 1993 he was heading its V8 engine program. He worked on Rover projects from 1995 to 1998, then returned to Munich as head of development for alternative combustion technologies. A series of executive positions in advanced engine development followed, and in 2005 he became head of Product Planning for all BMW Group brands, followed by even more responsibility as head of Brand and Product Strategies from 2007 to 2012.

Later that year, Fröhlich took charge of BMW's small and medium car development, leading the engineering team that transformed BMW's flaccid F30 3 Series into the much tighter, more responsive F32 4 Series coupe. That car launched just prior to Fröhlich's elevation to the board, suggesting that BMW was eager to follow his direction back to sportier, edgier

cars after a nearly a decade of moving in the opposite direction.

That included a third-generation Z4 roadster, which Fröhlich was determined to get built. "At the moment this segment is very small, and I had to fight hard to make the [new Z4] happen at all, honestly," Fröhlich told *Car and Driver* in 2019. "It was against the finance controllers."

Fröhlich got it into production thanks to development cost-sharing with Toyota, along with other important concessions. The car would be available in rear-wheel drive only, with just two engines, and with only one transmission. As with the E89 Z4, no M version would be offered.

Instead, the highest-performance Z4 would be from M Performance, the sub-brand that offered M styling enhancements with engines and suspensions tuned midway between those of a series-production BMW and a full-on M car.

M Performance six

Even if it wasn't a real M car, the Z4 M40i offered plenty of power from its B58 inline six-cylinder engine. As the "B" indicates, the all-aluminum B58 is part of a new generation of modular engines, with crankcases designed to be shared between gasoline- and diesel-burning engines alike. It uses a closed-deck engine block design—more expensive to build, but more durable, with fewer open spaces where the cylinder head meets the block. The design also allows the engine to make more power safely, or to accept higher boost pressures from the TwinScroll turbocharger. Displacing 2,998cc, the engine also features double VANOS, Valvetronic, direct fuel injection, and a water-cooled exhaust manifold integrated into the cylinder head. Output peaks at 382 horsepower between 5,000 and 6,500 rpm, plus 369 pound-feet from 1,600 to 4,500 rpm.

Delivered through the standard ZF eight-speed automatic, that's enough to propel the 3,443-pound Z4 roadster from zero to 60 mph in just 3.9 seconds. Top speed is electronically limited to 155 mph, which the Z4 40i can reach with ease thanks to a slippery Cd of 0.29 with its top up. Top down, aerodynamic efficiency falls to 0.35.

For those who didn't require such aggressive performance, BMW offers the Z4 30i. Despite its name, the car is powered by a 1,998cc B46 four-cylinder engine. With its block and head in aluminum, the B46 uses TwinPower turbocharging, Valvetronic, Double VANOS and High Precision injection to deliver 255 horsepower between 5,000 and 6,500 rpm, and 295 pound-feet from 1,550 up to 4,400 rpm. The 3,287-pound Z4 30i can run the zero to 60 mph sprint in a respectable 5.2 seconds—still sports-car quick if not earth-shatteringly fast.

BMW didn't provide torsional stiffness ratings for the CLAR platform, but it has provided some interesting data about the car's dimensions. "The proportions have grown in every area over its predecessor: 3.3 inches longer, 2.9 inches wider and 0.5 inches taller. The wheelbase has been shortened by 1.0 inch [to 97.2 inches] which, combined with the notably wider tracks (+3.86 inches in front and +2.45 inches in rear, for new measurements of 62.8 inches front/62.6 inches rear on the M40i, 0.9 inch wider on the 30i) and a perfect 50:50 weight distribution, all contribute to the much enhanced vehicle agility."

At the rear axle, the Z4 uses a new five-link suspension, the first such arrangement used on a BMW Roadster, here executed in aluminum and steel. Fröhlich had always been attentive to the connection between axles, suspension, and the car's body, and the Z4 got an oversized axle support and subframe, plus additional bracing connecting it to the body.

Up front, the Z4 rides on a new version of BMW's "double-joint spring strut suspension." The front axle attaches securely to the body, with a stout subframe and stiff mounting points for the aluminum control arms. That rigid connection is said to enhance vehicle acoustics along with cornering precision and steering feel.

As on all Z4s, steering is via Electric Power Steering. The G29's EPS features variable assist and a variable ratio, with a mean of 15:1. It was designed to offer both "precise feedback during cornering and effortless low-speed maneuvering."

In addition, the Z4 M40i receives M Performance enhancements that include Adaptive M Sport suspension, M Sport brakes, and an electronically controlled M Sport differential that uses an electric motor to equalize torque distribution between the rear wheels. A new Driving Experience Control switch allows the driver to choose between familiar Comfort, Sport, and Sport+ modes, the latter tailored to extract maximum performance from the wide rubber: 255/40R-18 front, and 275/40R-18 rear run-flat tires, mounted on 9.0 and 10.0 x 18-inch wheels.

Athletic and agile

In the final analysis, did it all add up to the sports car Fröhlich had promised to build? In some respects, certainly. *Car and Driver* called its engine "a honey... wonderfully smooth and willing to rev." Overall, the magazine deemed the Z4 M40i "a highly athletic and agile roadster in need of better steering." The magazine elaborated, suggesting that the effort to make the chassis as stiff as possible might have gone too far. "Finding the BMW's flow on a good road is elusive. Its ultra-reactive steering speaks in whispers and its rear end breaks loose with abrupt throttle inputs. At a more relaxed pace, you'll find ride compliance and a quiver-free structure. The only thing spoiling your sunbathing is a fair amount of wind turbulence swirling into the cabin over your shoulder."

Despite those criticisms, *Car and Driver* still dubbed it "the best Z4 ever," an opinion echoed by Britain's *Top Gear*, which found the Z4 M40i as capable as the M2, with more versatility and easier cruising when desired.

BMW's roadsters have come a long way since the Z4 1.9 debuted in 1996, and all that technology doesn't come cheap. At launch, the Z4 M40i carried a base price of $63,700, while the Z4 30i sold for $49,700. For those enamored with BMW's top-down two-seaters, however, it's well worth the money, just as it has been for the last 35 years.

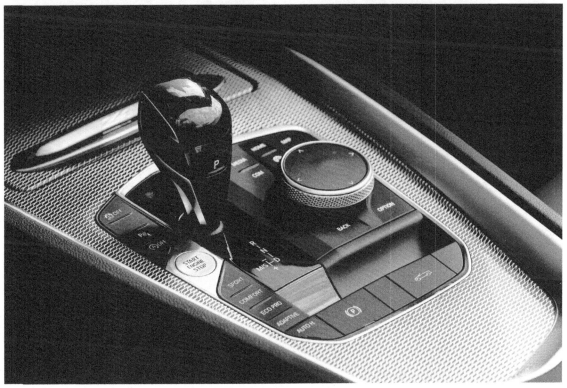

Made in the USA
Coppell, TX
09 December 2022

88346653R00092